STUDY GUIDE

S. ROSS DOUGHTY

Ursinus College

VOLUME II

THE
WORLD'S HISTORY

HOWARD SPODEK

PRENTICE HALL, *Upper Saddle River, New Jersey 07458*

© 1998 by PRENTICE-HALL, INC.
Simon & Schuster / A Viacom Company
Upper Saddle River, New Jersey 07458

ISBN 0-13-642828-2

Printed in the United States of America

CONTENTS
Volume II

INTRODUCTION
Volume II

To the student:

This *Study Guide* is intended to assist students in reading and understanding *The World's History*, by Howard Spodek. The *Guide* is therefore organized in the same format as the textbook, and naturally emphasizes the same themes and stresses the same historical issues as those of the author. If you have looked at the textbook, or even its table of contents, you will see that it is not arranged in the usual chronological-geographical framework of other world history texts, but rather employs a **thematic approach**. The two volumes are divided into eight thematic sections, each of which examines a specific topic within a broad time-span, ranging from millions of years (Part One) to several centuries (Chapter 12). Each section (with the exceptions of Parts One and Six) is then subdivided into two to six chapters, each of which examines a more specific topic, question or geographical area within the sectional theme. "World history," as presented and interpreted in the textbook, is both more and less than "the history of the world." It represents <u>less</u> than many novice students might expect, in that it makes no attempt at anything like the comprehensive narrative coverage found in many traditional surveys (which make it, among other things, a shorter book!). On the other hand, it also includes <u>more</u> than many, much weightier, more conventional texts, in that it interprets *The World's History* in a conceptual and comparative framework that is designed to make the story of our global development more comprehensible and more meaningful to students in introductory college courses.

This thematic and conceptual approach reflects the way in which historians approach their subject. History is not just the recording and retelling of myriad facts or interesting stories: the word "history" is derived from the Greek *iistoria*, meaning "inquiry" or research. It involves analyzing information and evidence (which historians usually call **sources**); posing and answering questions; and formulating, examining and revising our explanations and conclusions (which historians refer to as **interpretation**). All history is interpretation and, as Howard Spodek states in the Introduction to *The World's History*, interpretations are constantly being revised because both the questions historians ask and the evidence they use to answer those questions are constantly changing.

The textbook presents the story of global human existence in such a way as to emphasize the interpretive and analytical aspects of history. In each chapter, the author reiterates the questions, **"What do we know?"** and **"How do we know it?"** The student is therefore introduced not only to the historical narrative, but also to the **primary sources,** the contemporary evidence -- in the form of archeological artifacts, written documents, myths and legends, art, music, literature, architecture, and material goods of all kinds – which survives from the period and place under scrutiny. (A third question, **"What Difference Does it Make?"** or **"What Was Its Significance?"** is addressed throughout the second volume.) The text therefore emphasizes **historiography**: the way in which historians formulate and revise their interpretations and (often) critique each other's views. Spodek's sections also emphasize **comparative history** and **hypothesis testing**, the formation of "hypotheses based on general principles, and then testing them against comparative data from around the world" (Spodek, xxiii). The emphasis of the textbook then, is not on mere mastery of the historical narrative or details, but on critical reading, data analysis, question posing, and hypothesis testing, in a comparative global framework.

How to use this book:

The exercises in the *Study Guide* are designed to emphasize the same comparative, thematic approach and stress the same historiographical issues and hypotheses as those in the text. To get the most out of both *The World's History* and the *Study Guide*, students are encouraged first to read both the short introductory section to each chapter in the text and the "Commentary" section for that chapter in the *Guide*. Then read the assigned chapter, paying special attention to the questions that are asked and the hypotheses that are put forward ("What do we know?" – or think we know) as well as the evidence that is used to support those interpretations ("How do we know it?") – often presented in the shaded boxes. Also study the visual materials – the timeline, maps, photographs, sidebar charts, and "Spotlight" essays. Then proceed to the exercises and questions in the *Study Guide*. Some instructors may assign these as homework, pose some of the questions for class discussion or small-group work, or use some of the materials as the basis for quizzes or examination questions. But even if they do not, a thorough and conscientious approach to the various exercises will enable you to check your mastery of critical information and understanding of important issues and reinforce your learning and appreciation of the material presented in the textbook. Each chapter in the *Study Guide* is arranged as follows:

COMMENTARY

The chapter commentaries are meant to be neither summaries nor outlines. Rather, they are designed to highlight the thesis – or principal argument – of the chapter, in addition to explaining its major objectives, questions and themes and drawing comparisons with other chapters in the section. The commentaries are not meant to take the place of reading the chapter: they are merely intended to help students recognize the important issues and evidence as they are presented and relate it to material they have already learned. The terms in **boldface** type designate important concepts, persons, events, etc. (See the model presented on the previous page, which is, in fact, a commentary on the "Introduction" to *The World's History* – pp. xvii-xxv.)

CHAPTER OUTLINE

The chapter outlines are keyed to the headings of the main sections of each chapter (in red upper-case letters in the text) and their sub-sections (black upper-case and boldface letters in the text). These outlines are intentionally schematic, as they are not meant to take the place of reading the chapter. Their intended purpose is to serve as a guide to the flow and connections of the narrative and argument of each chapter and to provide a model framework for students taking notes from the text (which is highly recommended).

IDENTIFICATION TERMS

Each chapter of the *Study Guide* contains a list of ten terms, the knowledge and understanding of which are critical to the argument of the corresponding textbook chapter. The list is not meant to be comprehensive – other terms and concepts are reinforced in the multiple choice and study question sections – but tries to present a broad selection. Students are asked to provide a basic identification or definition for the term, an approximate date and geographical location and, more importantly, an explanation of the historical significance of the particular person, event, idea, movement, book, etc., in the context of the chapter. Page references from the text are provided for the student's use.

MULTIPLE CHOICE QUESTIONS

These are designed to test both mastery of the historical narrative and some of the important issues and concepts presented in the text. Students are asked to pick the response that best answers the question or completes the sentence. Some of them <u>are</u> tricky and are meant to be so, since they are intended to reinforce careful reading of the text. An answer key, with page references, is provided at the end of each chapter in the *Study Guide*. In some cases, the questions and answers are open to different interpretations: a student who disagrees with an answer in the *Guide* should raise the question with the instructor in class.

STUDY QUESTIONS

Each chapter contains 4-6 analytical or interpretive questions designed to provoke thought and discussion concerning some of the major questions or hypotheses in the textbook chapter. Sometimes a question might require a comparative analysis, based on material from a previous chapter as well. In any case, these questions all require that the student formulate an argument or test a hypothesis and provide concrete examples and evidence, presented in a concise and coherent way, to support his or her case. Sometimes students will even be required to go beyond the direct evidence that is presented in the text and make <u>inferences</u>, or educated guesses, based on what they do know. Since these questions can be rather subjective, different conclusions, based on differing interpretations of the evidence, are often possible.

HOW DO WE KNOW?

These questions are similar in nature to the Study Questions, except that they are all based directly on primary source evidence or historical interpretations which have been presented in the textbook chapter. The primary source evidence includes extracts or quotations from various written documents and photographs of visual sources, ranging from small objects, to paintings, to monumental structures. The historiographical sources may be found in the main text or in the "Spotlight" sections in the chapters. Again, students are often asked to make inferences regarding questions for which there may not be a definitive answer.

MAP ANALYSIS

This section includes simple map location exercises, which are designed to reinforce geographical knowledge and help students relate events and movements within their global setting, as well as more analytical and interpretive questions based on the many maps in each chapter. In some cases, even the location exercises will require a two-step process. Rather than asking you to find Timbuktu on a map, for example, you might be asked to "locate the most important center of Islamic learning in west Africa, c. 1400 C.E." Again, many of the more interpretive questions will require students to "go out on a limb" and make inferences based on fragmentary evidence or comparisons of several different maps. Outline maps of the regions discussed in the chapter are provided for students to work with. Many instructors may assign these exercises for homework or include them on quizzes.

12   ESTABLISHING WORLD TRADE ROUTES
1100 - 1500 C.E.

THE PATTERNS AND PHILOSOPHIES OF
EARLY ECONOMIC SYSTEMS

COMMENTARY

Part Five – *World Trade* – examines the importance of trade and economics in world history between (c. 1100-1800 and its role in the transmission and exchange of ideas, culture and even diseases, as well as material goods. Chapter 12 reviews the origins and development of world trade networks from approximately 1100 to 1500, C.E. The thesis – or principal argument – of the chapter is that long-distance trade, mostly in **luxury goods** for the wealthy or non-perishable bulk items such as raw wool or cotton, has formed a significant component of the world's economic systems from the earliest civilizations and that, by the beginning of the second millennium C.E., a number of flourishing, highly sophisticated – and mutually connected – **trading networks** had developed in China and southeast Asia, central and southwest Asia, the Indian Ocean littoral, sub-Saharan Africa and the Mediterranean basin. Similar trade patterns were established separately in the Americas as well, particularly in central America and the Andes region. The relatively impoverished regions of western and central Europe existed on the periphery of the Afro-Eurasian pattern of trade until a set of fortuitous climatic, social, religious and technological changes served to stimulate economic growth in Europe and eventually allowed Europeans to break out of their semi-isolation, thrust themselves into those long-established trade networks, and even link the eastern and western hemispheres after 1492.

As Chapter 12 demonstrates, the study of long-distance exchange is important to historians for a number of reasons. First, the amount and nature of the goods traded provides a good index of the prosperity of a given economy and fluctuations in long-distance trade are indicative of important developments in other aspects of society. Medieval Europe, for example, could not be an important player in world trade while it remained relatively underdeveloped and the Christian Church was hostile to the idea of individual profit. Second, trade has played an important role in linking distant regions and in fostering the migrations of peoples and ideas. The Chinese, Arab and Jewish **diasporas**, for example, as well as the spread of Hinduism, Buddhism, Christianity and Islam, have been fostered by traders. Thirdly, the study of world trade patterns helps us to understand that the economic goals, functions and priorities of different societies are by no means identical or even consistent. While **free market economies** based on private profit have existed in a number of places at different times, they have had to coexist with – and have often been superseded by – theories or systems which placed a higher value on the idea of a **"moral economy"** that guaranteed subsistence for all, or government-regulated economies which placed the welfare and security of the state above that of any group or individual.

The author outlines and compares the distinctive structures, major trade commodities and important developments in six major trading areas of the period: the Americas (including the Aztec and Inca trade networks); west and east Africa, south of the Sahara; the Indian Ocean trade system; the Mongol Empire; China and the South China Sea; and medieval Europe and the Mediterranean Sea. Several of these trade areas – most notably **Ming** China and the Aztec and Inca Empires -- were characterized by a high degree of state control over the economy, whereas others – particularly the Indian Ocean network and that of later medieval Europe – were tilted more toward private profit and a free market. China under the **Mongols** and the Ming Dynasty and medieval Europe are examined in the greatest detail, with implicit comparisons being made between the two. The major question addressed throughout the latter part of the chapter is why and how western Europe, an economic backwater at the beginning of the period, was able to become a dynamic trading power, while China, the world's largest and most vigorous economy, began to show signs of stagnation, relative to the western upstarts.

CHAPTER OUTLINE

A. Trade and Traders: Goals and Functions

    1. World trade: <u>What difference does it make?</u>
    2. Trade networks, 1250-1500

B. World Trade Patterns, 1100-1500: <u>What do we know?</u>

    1. The Americas
    2. Sub-Saharan Africa
        a. West Africa
        b. East Africa
    3. Indian Ocean Trade
        a. Jewish traders
        b. Muslim traders
    4. The military and trade empire of the Mongols
        a. Genghis Khan
        b. World travelers: Marco Polo and Ibn Battuta
        c. bubonic plague and the trade routes
    5. China and the South China Sea
        a. from Mongol to Ming: dynastic transition
        b. international trade and government intervention
    6. Medieval Europe and the Mediterranean, 700-1500
        a. the early Middle Ages
        b. the High Middle Ages
        c. the rise of an urban middle class
        d. the Church revises its economic policies
        e. guilds and city-states confront rural aristocrats
        f. economic and social conflict within the city
        g. the Renaissance: intellectual and cultural transformation
        h. ironies of the 14th century: plague and war
    7. The Rise of the Ottomans in Eastern Europe
    8. Exploration and discovery

IDENTIFICATION TERMS

For each term provide an identification or definition, an approximate date, a geographical location (if relevant) and – most important – a concise explanation of its significance in the context of the chapter. (Page numbers from the text are provided for your reference.)

pochteca (p. 362): guild of traders that carried on long-distance trade which expanded steadily thru the 15th century. Only marry within the guild Led caravans - knives, fur blankets - clothes, herbs, dyes - brought back jade, seashells, jaguar skins, + cotton from Gulf coast.

Genghis Khan (p. 370):

moral economy (p. 359): everyone within the village be fed before any individual is permitted to sell surplus food outside the village for private profit.

Mansa Musa (p. 365): Muslim emperor of Mali. 1324 passed through Cairo on his way to Mecca - he gave out so much gold that the value of Cairo's currency was depressed for many years.

Zheng He (p. 377):

"stranger merchants" (p. 359): cross cultural brokers, helping + encouraging trade between the host society + people of their own origin who moved along the trade routes. They formed a series of trade settlements in alien towns.

caravels (p. 388):

bubonic plague (p. 375, 390):

Great Zimbabwe (p. 365):

Renaissance humanism (p. 387):

MULTIPLE CHOICE QUESTIONS

Select the response that completes the sentence or answers the question best.

1. Which of the following developments was <u>not</u> a result or side-effect of economic recovery in medieval Europe?
   a. modification of Christian attitudes towards trade and profit
   b. a rise in class tensions between *bourgeois* employers and their employees
   c. greater tolerance towards Jews
   d. the granting of town charters by regional rulers

2. East Africa was brought into the Eurasian trading system in the 9th century by:
   a. the arrival of Arab merchants via the Indian Ocean
   b. the introduction of the camel
   c. the voyages of Admiral Zheng He
   d. the arrival of Portuguese explorers

3. In a completely "free market economy," prices would vary only according to:
   a. the location of the market
   b. the needs of the poor
   c. the relationship between the supply of goods and the demand for them
   d. the effort of the merchant

4. In the Inca Empire, the economic specialties of different regions were determined mainly by:
   a. their proximity to the Pacific Ocean
   b. the state and its semi-divine rulers
   c. the demands of Spanish traders
   d. their relative altitude in the Andes Mountains

5. The principal motivation of Portugal's Prince Henry the Navigator in fostering overseas exploration was:
   a. to spread Christianity in the New World
   b. to find a trade route to Asia free from control by the Ottoman Turks
   c. to prove that the earth was round
   d. all of the above

6. Which of the following European technological advance of the period 1100-1500 was <u>not</u> originally a European invention?
   a. gunpowder weapons
   b. the decimal system
   c. printing with movable type
   d. all of the above

7. In earlier times, luxury goods comprised the major portion of long-distance trade because:
   a. of their value relative to their weight
   b. they were in heavy demand
   c. they were bartered in exchange for other goods
   d. their transportation costs were subsidized by regional rulers

8. Under the Mongol and Ming dynasties in China, the principal producers of cotton cloth were:
   a. urban guild members
   b. government slaves
   c. rural peasant women
   d. Jewish merchants

9. The most noteworthy cultural and intellectual achievements of the Italian Renaissance occurred in Florence, under the patronage of:
   a. Niccolo Machiavelli
   b. the Medici family
   c. the *Ciompi*
   d. Leonardo da Vinci

10. The most likely purpose of the seven voyages of the Chinese admiral Zheng He was:
    a. to establish new trade routes free from Mongol control
    b. to collect tribute from rulers and trading cities along the routes of the expeditions
    c. to extend the political control of the Ming Emperor
    d. to seek new markets for Chinese goods

11. The best examples of governments which derived their power and wealth by controlling traders and trade routes, rather than land and agriculture, during the period covered in the chapter, were:
    a. the Aztec and Inca empires of the Americas
    b. the feudal kingdoms of western Europe
    c. the Mongol khanates
    d. Ghana, Mali and Songhai in west Africa

12. The anthropologists Karl Polanyi and James Scott are closely identified with the study of which of the following:
    a. the concept of the "moral economy of the poor"
    b. the "law of supply and demand"
    c. *Realpolitik* (the argument that "the ends justify the means")
    d. the development of pre-modern trading networks

13. Which of the following areas was never successfully conquered by the Mongols?
    a. China
    b. Japan
    c. Iraq
    d. Russia

14. Which of the following groups was not a part of the "feudal" economic and political system of medieval Europe?
    a. lords of the manor
    b. vassals
    c. serfs
    d. guilds

15. An unintended consequence of the *Pax Mongolica*, or "Mongol Peace" may have been:
    a. the introduction of the camel into North Africa
    b. the introduction of feudalism into Europe
    c. the introduction of the bubonic plague into Europe
    d. the decline of trade between China and central Asia

STUDY QUESTIONS

Consider each of the following questions carefully. Be prepared to supply specific evidence and examples to support your points in a class discussion or a concise, well-organized written essay.

1. According to the author of the text, "All societies … regulate trade to some degree in order also to serve the non-economic goals of the society. Business may be more or less regulated, but it is never completely unregulated" (Spodek, p. 358). Cite at least three examples of such regulation from the chapter. In each case, who was actually regulating trade and how? What "non-economic goals" were being served?

2. From approximately 750 to 1500 C.E., central Asian, trans-Saharan and Indian Ocean trade routes were dominated by Muslim traders, mostly Arabs, Berbers and Persians. What are the most likely reasons for this Muslim dominance? What were some of its principal effects? Cite specific examples from the text.

3. Between 1407 and 1433, the Ming Emperor of China sent his great Admiral Zheng He on seven great seaborne expeditions, extending as far as India, the Persian Gulf and east Africa. But the voyages were discontinued and never followed up by the extension of Chinese political or commercial control to those areas, in spite of the fact that China was probably the richest and most powerful country in the world. Why was this the case? And what, according to many historians, were some of the consequences of this withdrawal?

4. The chapter discusses no fewer than five important social, political and cultural consequences of the flowering of the European economy from the 11th through the 15th centuries C.E. List as many of these consequences as you can and then review at least two of them in detail, explaining specifically how economic growth brought about the political, social or cultural change under discussion.

5. Compare the flourishing economies of Mongol and Ming China with that of later medieval and Renaissance Europe. In what ways were they similar? In what ways did they differ? Are there any indications in the text that the European economy might overtake that of China in the period after 1500?

6. According to the text, Jews had become "so much a part of the merchant classes in early medieval northern Europe that a traditional administrative phrase referred to 'Jews and other merchants' " (Spodek, p. 383). Why was this the case? In what respects were Jews the classical "stranger merchants" referred to earlier in the chapter (p. 359)? What were the effects of this on the status of Jews in Christian Europe?

HOW DO WE KNOW?

The following questions are based on the various illustrations or quotations and extracts from primary source documents and historical interpretations in the chapter.

1. In the extract from the *Summa Theologica* by St. Thomas Aquinas (p. 384), the text cites evidence of a major revision of the policies of the Christian Church regarding business and trade. What had been the earlier view of the Church? How does Aquinas reflect a rethinking of the Christian position? What may have been some of the reasons for this change? What were some of the consequences for the Church; for traders and businessmen; and for Jews in Europe?

2. What inferences and generalizations about long-distance trade can you make on the basis of the fragmentary excerpts from the *Rihla* of the Muslim traveler Ibn Battuta and the *Travels of Marco Polo* (pp. 373-74)? How might they support some of the major points made in the chapter?

3. The two facets of feudalism – political and economic – are illustrated in the print from the *British Museum* (p. 379) and the extract from Louis the Pious's *Capitulare de Villis* (p. 380). What generalizations and inferences can be made about feudalism, vassalage and the manorial economy from these contemporary sources?

4. Based on the extracts from *The Travels of Marco Polo* (pp. 375 & 377) and the poems by Dong Xianliang and Xu Xianzhong (pp. 375-376), what was the "underside" of Chinese economic growth under the Mongol and Ming dynasties? Who were the "winners" and "losers" in the Chinese economy of the time?

MAP ANALYSIS

The following exercise is based on the maps on pp. 360, 364, 370, and 372.

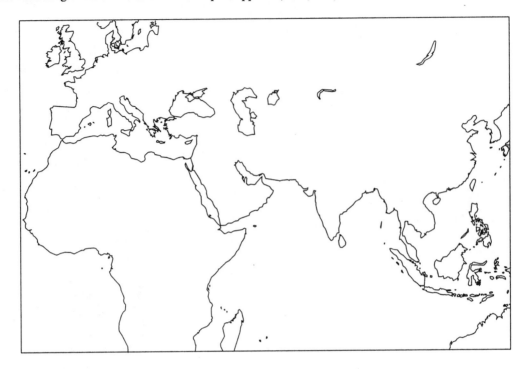

1. On the map above, locate and label the following:
    a. the major land and sea trade routes of Eurasia and Africa
    b. the major trading kingdoms of Africa
    c. the approximate boundaries of the Mongol Empire at its greatest extent and those of its "Successor States"
    d. the major routes followed by the spread of bubonic plague (the "Black Death")
    e. Hangzhou, Guangzhou, Malacca, Calicut, Zanzibar, Sofala, Baghdad, Venice, Genoa, Fez, and Timbuktu

2. Compare the map of "World Trade Routes" (p. 360) with that of "The Routes of the Plague" (p. 372). What obvious inferences can be drawn from this comparison?

3. What was the effect of the "Pax Mongolica" on Eurasian trade? How do the travels of Ibn Battuta and Marco Polo illustrate this?

MULTIPLE CHOICE ANSWER KEY (with page references)

1.	C	(384)	6.	D	(385)	11.	D	(363)
2.	A	(365)	7.	A	(356)	12.	A	(358)
3.	C	(358)	8.	C	(376)	13.	B	(371)
4.	D	(360)	9.	B	(388)	14.	D	(386)
5.	B	(390)	10.	B	(378)	15.	C	(375)

13   THE UNIFICATION OF WORLD TRADE
1500 – 1776

THE INVISIBLE HAND REACHES OUT:
A CAPITALIST WORLD SYSTEM APPEARS

COMMENTARY

The previous chapter surveyed the development of trading networks in Asia, Africa, the Indian Ocean, Europe and the Mediterranean, and the Americas, as well as the different social, religious and political foundations on which the economies of those areas were based. Chapter 13 examines the emergence of a unified system of world trade which, for the first time, was to knit those various regional networks together into single, global network. This new **world system** was characterized by two distinctive features. First, it was based on **capitalism**, that is on the "private ownership of wealth and the **means of production** and on the pursuit of private economic profit" (Spodek, 394). Also, it was dominated by European traders, bankers, entrepreneurs and plantation owners who, with the encouragement, financial support and naval protection of their countries' increasingly powerful, centralized governments, wrested control of much of the world's trade from the former regional networks and redirected it for their own profit, while bringing many regions of the Americas, Asia and Africa under their imperial rule.

Because of this European domination, the chapter focuses on the development of the European powers, the expansion of their trading empires, and their increasingly aggressive and expensive rivalry for economic profit and control of the lion's share of the world's trade. A closely-related theme is the gradual evolution of capitalist enterprise in practice and eventually as a fully-articulated (though as yet unnamed) theory in *The Wealth of Nations* (1776), by the Scottish philosopher and economist **Adam Smith**. A number of important questions relating to these topics are addressed. What internal political, social, religious and economic factors within the five European trading states (Portugal, Spain, the Netherlands, France and England) contributed to their rather sudden emergence as expansionist powers? How were they able to extend their domination over such vast areas in so short a period of time? What was the nature of the relationship between private enterprise and the government in each of those states? Why did the Dutch, the French, and eventually the British ultimately surpass Spain and Portugal as imperial powers? What were the effects of European domination on the regions and peoples they controlled? And how and why were some areas, such as Russia, the **Ottoman Empire**, China, and **Tokugawa Japan**, able to stave off economic encroachment by western Europe?

The author's answers to these questions necessitate a brief discussion of a number of important contemporary developments, among them the rise of the Spanish monarchy, the **Protestant Reformation**, the **Dutch Revolt**, royal absolutism and **mercantilism** under **Louis XIV** of France, and agricultural **enclosures** and the establishment of the **Bank of England** in Britain. Although these topics may appear at first to have little or nothing to do with world trade, they are, in fact, critical to understanding how western Europe, a relatively small and heretofore backward corner of the Eurasian land-mass, could come to control so much territory and manipulate so much of the world's wealth.

On the question of the effects of this European-dominated capitalist system, within Europe itself and around the world, the text attempts to present a balanced assessment. While there were some clear "winners" and "losers" in the process – European merchant classes in general and Britain, in particular, among the former; and the native American peoples and African slaves among the latter – in other places the results were not so unambiguous. The population grew and the standard of living improved over much of Europe after 1700, yet the vigorously entrepreneurial merchant castes of India also thrived during the period. And while Portugal and Spain were ultimately bankrupted by the costs of their wars and distant empires, the merchants and government of **Qing Dynasty** China reaped handsome profits for their controlled trade with Europe. As the text points out, much of the silver and gold that were mined from Mexico and Peru found its way to China, where it was exchanged for fine porcelain, silk and tea.

CHAPTER OUTLINE

A. Capitalism and the Expansion of Europe
    1. Capitalism: a definition
    2. European capitalism and the expansion of trade: <u>What difference does it make?</u>

B. Spain's Empire
    1. New World conquests
    2. Making the conquests pay
    3. Merchant profits
    4. Warfare and bankruptcy

C. Trade and Religion in Europe: the Protestant Reformation and the Catholic Counter-Reformation
    1. The Reformation
    2. The Counter-Reformation
    3. Religious beliefs and capitalist practice
    4. Protestant challenges from the Dutch Republic and England

D. Portugal's Empire
    1. Sugar, slaves, and food
    2. The Indian Ocean: advancing Portugal's coastal explorations of Africa
    3. How significant were the Portuguese?

E. The Dutch Republic

F. France and England
    1. France: consolidating the nation
    2. Britain: establishing commercial supremacy
        a. British triumph in overseas trade: <u>What do we know and how do we know?</u>
        b. agriculture in economic growth

G. Capitalism

H. Diverse Cultures: Diverse Economic Systems
    1. Russia
    2. Ottomans and Mughals
    3. Ming and Qing dynasties in China
    4. Tokugawa Japan
    5. Southeast Asia

IDENTIFICATION TERMS

     For each term provide an identification or definition, an approximate date, a geographical location (if relevant) and – most important – a concise explanation of its significance in the context of the chapter. (Page numbers from the text are provided for your reference.)

enclosures (pp. 416-417):

Edo (p. 426):

indulgences (p. 400):

encomienda **system** (p. 398):

Dutch East India Company (p. 409-410):

theories of modernization and dependency (p. 395):

Jesuits (pp. 402; 423-425):

mercantilism (p. 414):

asiento (p. 414):

St. Petersburg (pp. 420-421):

MULTIPLE CHOICE QUESTIONS

Select the response that completes the sentence or answers the question best.

1. The German sociologist Max Weber argued, in effect, that:
    a. the spirit of capitalism promoted Protestantism in Europe
    b. the teachings of Protestantism promoted capitalism in Europe
    c. the expansion of capitalism promoted modernization outside of Europe
    d. the expansion of capitalism promoted dependency outside of Europe

2. Which of the following economic enterprises in the Americas was fought over the most by European powers?
    a. the Canadian fur trade
    b. trade with the Spanish colonies in Latin America
    c. the West Indies slave trade
    d. trade with the British colonies in North America

3. Which of the following best describes Adam Smith's view of the proper role of the government in a country's economy?
    a. total *laissez-faire* – that is, no government intervention at all
    b. the provision of tax incentives and other forms of support for joint-stock companies
    c. the maintenance of import restrictions and other mercantilist policies to protect business
    d. spending for public works and the enforcement of laws to protect the workings of the market

4. It is estimated that between one-third and one-half of all the silver mined in Spanish America between 1527 and 1821 ultimately ended up in:
    a. China, as payment for Chinese silk, porcelain and tea
    b. Britain, as booty captured from Spanish treasure fleets
    c. Antwerp, as interest on loans to the Spanish monarchy from Flemish bankers
    d. Rome, as contributions to the Papacy's struggle against the Protestant reformation

5. The economic policies followed by Czar Peter the Great of Russia most closely resembled those of:
    a. the Dutch East India Company
    b. the Tokugawa *shoguns* of Japan
    c. the Mughal emperors of India
    d. Louis XIV and his minister Colbert, in France

6. How did the Catholic Church respond to the challenge of the Protestant Reformation?
    a. by sending missionaries to convert non-Christians in Asia, Africa and the Americas
    b. by reaffirming the basic doctrines of Catholicism
    c. by establishing new religious orders and reforming church practices
    d. all of the above

7. Martin Luther's opposition to the sale of indulgences by the church was based primarily on:
    a. his acceptance of St. Paul's doctrine of justification (salvation) by faith alone
    b. his opposition to clerical marriage
    c. his outrage at the wealth and corruption of the Catholic Church
    d. his support for the German princes

8. Which of the following was <u>not</u> a reason why the Ming Dynasty lost the "Mandate of Heaven" and was overthrown, according to the text?
    a. failure to control piracy on the coasts and rivers of China
    b. invasion by Manchus from north of the Great Wall
    c. failure to control the activities of Portuguese traders
    d. deteriorating quality of imperial officials

9. The economic fortunes of the Ottoman Empire during the period covered in the chapter most closely resembled those of:
    a. the Mughal Empire in India
    b. the Spanish monarchy
    c. France under Louis XIV
    d. China under the Qing Dynasty

10. The term "development of underdevelopment" refers to:
    a. the short-sighted economic policies resorted to by Ottoman, Chinese and Japanese rulers in the 1600's
    b. the unequal distribution of the world's wealth, brought about by European economic dominance
    c. the failure of Spain and Portugal to keep up with the Dutch, French and British after 1600
    d. all of the above

11. Adam Smith used the term "the invisible hand" to refer to:
    a. the role of competition in a free-market economy
    b. the role of government in a free-market economy
    c. the role of government-sponsored monopolies like the British East India Company
    d. the Law of Accumulation

12. The main motivation behind the Spanish and Portuguese voyages of exploration was:
    a. the desire to convert Asian peoples to Catholic Christianity
    b. the desire to prove that Europeans could reach Asia by sailing west
    c. the desire to find a trade route to Asia independent of Ottoman control
    d. the desire to dominate the African slave trade

13. China and Japan pursued similar strategies in dealing with European traders, by:
    a. totally closing off their countries to Europeans
    b. allowing only European joint stock companies to trade in their countries
    c. restricting Europeans to small trading enclaves in their ports
    d. requiring that all European trade be conducted by their own merchants and ships

14. Which of the following was <u>not</u> a cause of the decline of Spain in the 17th century?
    a. the cost of Spain's wars against the Dutch and other European Protestants
    b. the fact that much of the trade with her American colonies was controlled by other countries
    c. the fact that the successors of Charles V and Philip II were incompetent rulers
    d. the fact that oppressive Spanish rule caused revolts in her American colonies

15. Which of the following best describes the motivation of King Henry VIII of England for breaking with the Roman Catholic Church?
    a. the desire to take control of the Catholic Church in England
    b. the desire to establish the Protestant religion in England
    c. the desire to help the Dutch Revolt against Spain
    d. the desire to establish a divine-right monarchy in England

STUDY QUESTIONS

Consider each of the following questions carefully. Be prepared to supply specific evidence and examples to support your points in a class discussion or concise, well-organized written essay.

1. Discuss the Spanish conquest of the Aztec and Incan civilizations of Mexico and Peru, with particular reference to two questions. First, how were a mere handful of Spanish *conquistadors* able to subdue these two powerful empires in so brief a period of time? And second, how did the Spanish exploit those peoples for their own – and Europe's – profit, in succeeding years?

2. Based on what you have learned from Chapters 12 and 13, what were the principal causes of the Protestant Reformation? What were the major objections raised by Luther, Calvin and other reformers against Catholic doctrines and practices? Why were the reformers able to gain such widespread acceptance in some areas of Europe but not in others?

3. In some ways the decline of the Spanish monarchy parallels the classic model of imperial decay, as outlined in Chapter 5 (pp. 114-115). Using the model presented in that chapter and specific evidence and examples from Chapter 13, explain why the Spanish Empire began to decline, c. 1570-1700.

4. Compare the reasons for the rise of France and the Dutch Republic as major trading powers in the 17th century. What advantages did they enjoy that Spain and Portugal did not? Conversely, what weaknesses began to show in their political or economic systems which later put them at a disadvantage in the face of competition from Britain?

5. Why was a free market economy the best system of exchange, according to Adam Smith? Why was *laissez-faire* preferable to regulation by church or state? How would individual or corporate greed be controlled under such a system, according to Smith? How does Smith's system compare with the older European view of a "moral economy of the poor?" (See Chapter 12.)

6. Compare the responses of the governments of the Ottoman and Mughal Empires, the Ming and Qing Dynasties in China, and Tokugawa Japan, to the encroachment of European economic and naval power in their respective territories. Why were China and Japan more successful than the two Muslim empires in holding the Europeans at bay?

The following questions are based on the illustrations or quotations and extracts from primary source documents and historical interpretations in the chapter.

1. How does the French historian Fernand Braudel, in *Civilization and Capitalism 15th-18th Century*, account for the success of Great Britain in establishing the largest and most enduring economic empire of all the European powers?

2. How might the term "quixotic" – derived from Miguel de Cervantes' novel *Don Quixote de la Mancha* – be applied to the role of Spain, and particularly its monarchy and nobility, in the 16th and 17th centuries?

MAP ANALYSIS

The following exercises are based on the maps on pp. 360, 406, 408 and 415.

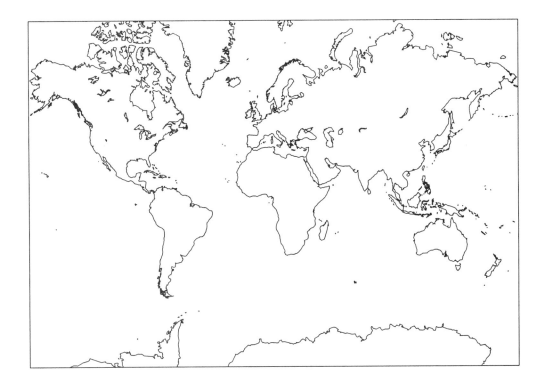

1. On the map above, locate and identify the following:
    a. the major trade routes of the first European trading empires
    b. the different territories controlled by the European powers, c. 1750
    c. the relative locations of the Ottoman and Mughal Empires
    d. "New France", Diu, Deshima, Batavia, Elmina, Calcutta, Manila

2. Compare the maps on pages 360 and 406. What generalizations can one make regarding changes in the patterns of world trade between c. 1450 (p. 360) and c. 1750 (p. 406)?

MULTIPLE CHOICE ANSWER KEY (with page references)

1.	B	(407)	6.	D	(402)	11.	A	(419)
2.	C	(414)	7.	A	(400)	12.	B	(421)
3.	D	(419)	8.	C	(423-425)	13.	C	(425)
4.	A	(399)	9.	B	(421)	14.	D	(400; 403-404)
5.	D	(420-421)	10.	B	(395)	15.	A	(401)

PART
6

Migration:
Free People
and
Slaves

1500 – 1750

"BE FRUITFUL AND MULTIPLY,
FILL UP THE EARTH AND SUBDUE IT":
DEMOGRAPHIC CHANGES IN A NEW GLOBAL ECUMENE

14   DEMOGRAPHY AND MIGRATION
1500 – 1750

THE MOVEMENT OF PEOPLES
AROUND THE EARTH

COMMENTARY

Chapter 14 comprises its own section – *Migration: Free Peoples and Slaves* – focusing on the core period of the great movement of peoples within Eurasia and across the oceans that began with the Turks and the Mongols in the 13th century (see Chapter 12) and continued through the huge emigration of Europeans to the "New World" in the 18th and 19th. Five different migrations and their results are examined in the chapter. The first four are movements of peoples: the migration of nomadic Turks and Mongols, culminating in the consolidation and expansion of the **Ottoman, Safavid,** and **Mughal** empires; the establishment of European – principally English – settlement colonies in the Americas, southern Africa and the **Antipodes** (Australia and New Zealand); the internal migrations to the great imperial capitals of Istanbul, Isfahan, Delhi, and London; and the forced migration of some ten million Africans to the mines and plantations of America via the **slave trade**. The fifth "migration" was the **"Columbian Exchange"** or cross-migration of plants, animals, and diseases between the "Old" and "New" worlds. These topics are examined using the techniques of **demography**, the quantitative study of aggregate population patterns (birth and death rates, life expectancy, urban growth, etc.) by social scientists, in order to illustrate how historians try to determine the cumulative effects of the great population shifts of the period.

The three Asian empires shared several common features. All were multiethnic monarchies, dominated by a nomadic warrior elite, exhibiting varying degrees of cultural adaptation and **syncretism**. All were Muslim in religion, but included sizable non-Muslim populations, as well as dissident Islamic groups. All three developed social and political institutions from what had essentially been a tribal, warrior society: none ever really established a peaceful system of royal succession, for example, and the physical layout of the Safavid and Mughal capitals was modeled on that of a nomadic military camp. Finally, all three had to deal simultaneously with the problems of urbanization and economic change, as well as the arrival of aggressive European traders.

The "expansion of Europe" and the coerced **diaspora** of Africans represent the most obvious examples of the great migration of peoples, plants, animals and microbes that took place during the period c. 1500-1800. Everywhere the Europeans settled, they imported Eurasian crops (sugar, cotton, wheat), animals (horses, cattle, sheep) and farming methods. They also brought new diseases (smallpox, plague, influenza, and others), against which the native peoples of the Americas, South Africa, Australia and New Zealand had no natural immunity. The **indigenous** populations of those areas were decimated by disease, the loss of farming and hunting lands to the Europeans, the rigors of forced labor in mines and on plantations, and merciless warfare by the invader-settlers. To replace the lost labor of the native population, the Europeans brought millions of African slaves to work the sugar, tobacco and cotton plantations of the New World. At the same time, the European population began to grow rapidly, stimulated in part by the intensive cultivation of new crops such as potatoes and **maize** (corn) from the Americas and the economic development that was partially a consequence of colonization. This European population boom, in turn, triggered a number of other consequences, two of which were increased **urbanization** and further, massive, overseas emigration.

A number of questions relating to these topics are addressed in this and succeeding chapters. How well did the nomadic Turkish and Mongol warriors adapt to their new roles? What were the characteristic features and role of the new urban centers in Asia and Europe? What factors motivated European settlement and the brutal European treatment of the peoples of Africa, the Americas, and the Antipodes? Where and how did the slave traders acquire their cargoes? Where were most of the slaves sent and what conditions did they experience in shipment and after their arrival? And what, ultimately, were the cumulative demographic, economic, and political consequences of these five migrations within each of the five continents and on global developments up to the present day?

CHAPTER OUTLINE

A. Demography: <u>What is it and what are its uses?</u>

B. Asian Migrations, 1250-1600
   1. The Ottoman Empire, 1300-1700
   2. India: the Mughal Empire, 1526-1750
   3. Akbar's reign: <u>How do we know?</u>
   4. Safavid Persia, 1500-1700
   5. China: the Ming and Manchu dynasties, 1368-1750

C. Global Population Growth and Shift

D. Fernand Braudel and the *Annales* School of History

E. The Expansion of Europe, 1096-1750
   1. The "Columbian Exchange"
   2. The Antipodes: Australia and New Zealand, 1600-1900
   3. South Africa, 1652-1902

F. Slavery: Enforced Migration, 1500-1750
   1. How many slaves? <u>How do we know?</u>
   2. Reinterpreting the slave trade: <u>What is its significance?</u>
   3. The plantation system

G. Cities and Demographics
   1. Delhi/Shahjahanabad
   2. Isfahan
   3. Istanbul/Constantinople
   4. London

IDENTIFICATION TERMS

For each term provide an identification or definition, an approximate date, a geographical location (if relevant) and – most important – a concise explanation of its significance in the context of the chapter. (Page numbers from the text are provided for your reference.)

Shah Jahan (pp. 454-456):

Maoris (pp. 444-446):

Timur (Tamerlane) (pp. 436-437):

Isfahan (pp. 437; 456):

"Columbian Exchange" (p. 442):

James Cook (p. 444):

Babur (p. 436):

Istanbul (pp. 457-458):

Annales School (pp. 440-441):

Senegambia (pp. 450; 454):

MULTIPLE CHOICE QUESTIONS

Select the response that completes the sentence or answers the question best.

1. The English demographer E. A. Wrigley estimates that in 1750, London had a population of approximately 675,000, or ____ per cent of England's population.
    a. 51%
    b. 26%
    c. 11%
    d. 1%

2. Aurangzeb (1658-1707) pushed the boundaries of the Mughal Empire to their farthest extent, but also aroused much opposition within India because of the human and financial costs of his military campaigns and:
    a. his intolerant religious policies
    b. the expense of his lavish building in Agra
    c. his suppression of the Hindi language
    d. his alliances with European traders

3. The first European colony in Australia was established at Botany Bay:
    a. by the Portuguese, as a trading port
    b. by the French, as a naval base
    c. by Dutch Boers, or farmers
    d. by the English, as a penal colony

4. Which of the following areas imported the greatest number of African slaves to work its plantations?
    a. the French colony of Saint-Domingue (Haiti)
    b. the Spanish island of Cuba
    c. the English colonies of North America (later the United States)
    d. the Portuguese colony of Brazil

5. An important component of the armies of the Ottoman Empire were the regiments of _____, slave soldiers captured from among the Christian population of the Balkan Peninsula.
    a. *gazis*
    b. Sufis
    c. janissaries
    d. Serbs

6. It is estimated that, by 1750, the native population of the Americas, which is thought to have been approximately 30-50 million people in 1500, had been reduced by:
    a. 90 %
    b. 50%
    c. 25%
    d. 10%

7. Which of the following was not typical of the great imperial capital cities of the period, c. 1500-1750?
    a. they were enhanced by government building programs and merchant and noble residences
    b. they became manufacturing centers
    c. they attracted immigrants from different regions of their empires
    d. they became centers for the exchange of diverse ideas and traditions

8. Urdu, the "camp language" of the Mughal Empire, is a combination of Hindi, Persian and _____ elements.
   a. Mongol
   b. Arabic
   c. Turkish
   d. Chinese

9. A major difference between the African slave populations in tropical regions of the Americas and those in Britain's North American colonies (later the United States) was that:
   a. the North American slaves never worked on sugar plantations
   b. the North American slaves came from different parts of Africa
   c. the North American slave population was freed sooner
   d. the North American slave population grew through natural population growth

10. The Ottoman Sultan Mehmed II earned the nickname "The Conqueror" because of his conquest of::
    a. the Safavid Empire
    b. the Mamelukes of Egypt
    c. the city of Constantinople
    d. the Habsburg territory of Hungary

11. The population of Europe was at its largest, relative to the population of the rest of the world, in which of the following years?
    a. 1500
    b. 1700
    c. 1800
    d. 1900

12. The official state religion of the Persian Safavid Empire was:
    a. Hinduism
    b. Zoroastrianism
    c. Shi'a Islam
    d. Sunni Islam

13. The Qing Dynasty was established in China in 1644 by:
    a. Mongol invaders
    b. a peasant rebel leader
    c. Manchu invaders
    d. a former Ming Dynasty general

14. Which of the following important crops did not originate the Western Hemisphere?
    a. sugar
    b. potatoes
    c. tobacco
    d. maize (corn)

15. The American historian Philip Curtin has argued that population loss in Africa due to the slave trade was minimized somewhat, owing to the fact that:
    a. many of the slave traders were African themselves
    b. only about a third of the slaves sold out of Africa were women
    c. the European slave traders were careful not to take too many slaves from the same area
    d. much of Africa was overpopulated at the time

STUDY QUESTIONS

Consider each of the following questions carefully. Be prepared to supply specific evidence and examples to support your points in a class discussion or concise, well-organized written essay.

1. The text attributes much of the success of the Mughal Empire under Akbar to the emperor's policy of cultural syncretism. What is "syncretism"? What forms did this policy assume under Akbar and how did it contribute to his success in ruling India?

2. Describe the essential elements of the plantation system. In what respects did it, as Philip Curtin has argued, represent elements of both medieval European feudalism and the capitalist factory system?

3. By 1900, the number of Europeans (in Europe and elsewhere) was greater, relative to other peoples, than it had been at any other time or would be at any time in the future. What were the reasons for this?

4. According to Philip Curtain, "Rather than sustaining the regular excess of deaths over births typical of tropical America, the North American colonies developed a pattern of natural growth among the slaves … ." (*The Atlantic Slave Trade,* p. 73.) Discuss the possible reasons for this difference.

HOW DO WE KNOW?

The following questions are based on the various illustration or quotations and extracts from primary source documents and historical interpretations in the chapter.

1. Discuss the various historical opinions regarding the effects of the slave trade on Africa and African development. What role did Africans and African states play in the trade?

2. Compare the observations of the Arab historian and social philosopher Ibn Khaldun (p. 455) with the actual historical "life-cycle" of the three Muslim empires discussed in this chapter. In what respects does he appear to have been accurate in his observations, even though he wrote several centuries before the height of the power of the Ottomans, the Mughals and the Safavids?

3. Compare the three illustrations relating to the slave trade and plantation system on pp. 452-453. What message is each artist or illustrator attempting to convey? What techniques are used to convey that message?

4. How did the growth and development of London differ from that of other imperial capital cities discussed in the chapter? In what respects, according to E.A. Wrigley, might London's growth during the seventeenth century have been a "significant factor in giving birth to the industrialization of the eighteenth" century (Spodek, p.458)?

MAP ANALYSIS

A. The following exercise is based on the map on p. 448.

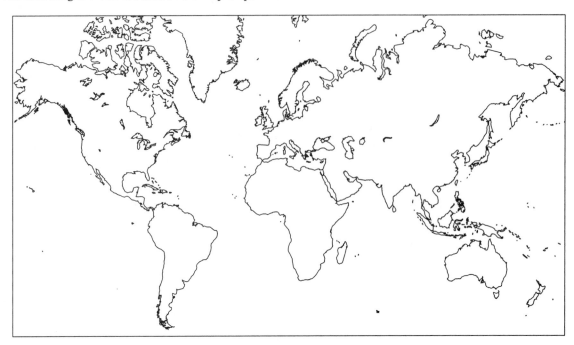

1. On the map above, locate and identify the principal slave settlement areas and those areas which were the principal sources of slaves. Which areas imported the most slaves?

2. Locate the major ports connected with the slave trade in Europe, Africa, Asia and the Americas.

B. The following exercise is based on the maps on pp. 431 and 433.

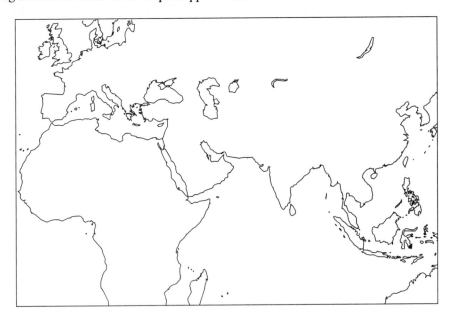

On the map above, locate and identify the following:
    1.   the boundaries of the Ottoman, Safavid, Mughal and Chinese Empires, c. 1300-1700
    2.   the regions of the Balkans, Serbia, Hungary, Syria, Persia, Gujarat, Punjab, and Bengal
    3.   the cities of Istanbul, Delhi, Agra, Samarkand, and Teheran
    4.   the battle-sites of Kosovo, Mohacs, Diu, Lepanto and Vienna

MULTIPLE CHOICE ANSWER KEY (with page references)

1.	C	(458)	6.	A	(442)	11.	D	(439)
2.	A	(434)	7.	B	(458)	12.	C	(437)
3.	D	(441)	8.	B	(434-436)	13.	D	(438)
4.	D	(449)	9.	D	(450)	14.	A	(442)
5.	C	(432)	10.	C	(432)	15.	B	(450)

PART
7

Social Change

1688 – 1914

WESTERN REVOLUTIONS AND THEIR EXPORT

POLITICAL REVOLUTIONS

15   IN EUROPE AND THE AMERICAS
1688 – 1850

THE BIRTH OF HUMAN RIGHTS
IN THE AGE OF ENLIGHTENMENT

COMMENTARY

Part Five, entitled *Social Change: Western Revolutions and Their Export*, contains three chapters, the first of which – Chapter 15 – is a comparative study of five significant political revolutions that occurred in Europe and the Americas between 1688 and 1850. The second chapter in the section examines the "Industrial Revolution", which began in Britain in the mid-18th century and spread to western Europe, the United States, and around the globe in the 19th and 20th centuries. Chapter 17 explores some of the momentous social effects of what has been called "The "Age of Revolution." "A **revolution**," Spodek states in the introduction to Chapter 15, "is a fundamental and often rapid change in the way systems operate – whether political, economic, intellectual or social" (p. 462). The political upheavals discussed in this chapter, for example, did not just result in changes in the leadership of the countries involved, such as might be the case when the Manchu Qing Dynasty replaced the Ming Dynasty in China in 1644. They represented much deeper changes in the political structure of Britain, her American colonies and France, changes in the "fundamental basis" of authority and the avowed purpose and goals of the government. Similarly, the "Industrial Revolution" was not revolutionary simply because it resulted in the production of more goods, or because those products were made using machinery. It was revolutionary because it brought about profound changes in the entire structure of the world's economy and society.

Chapter 15 begins with a general overview of political revolutions and a discussion of the common characteristics of the three major revolutions of the period: the **"Glorious Revolution"** (1688-89) in England, the **American Revolution** and War of Independence from Britain (1775-1783), and the **French Revolution** (1789-1799). As the text states, all three were "democratic" in the sense that they tended to increase popular participation in the government and claimed to establish governments of, for, and by "the people" -- or at least <u>more</u> of "the people" than had previously been the case. In so doing, they rejected the so-called **Divine Right of Kings**, replacing it with the concept of **government by consent of the governed** and a belief in "inalienable" **individual rights**. At the same time, however, all three revolutions sought to protect **private property**, while also promoting the power and efficiency of the state. These were potentially incompatible ideals, as the author notes, and were to lead to considerable conflict in the revolutionary period, especially in France. (Another such conflict was to become the cause of the American Civil War. What if, for example, one's property included slaves? Did the state have the power to free them?)

In addition to tracing how each of the three revolutions attempted to implement its ideals – and the degree to which it succeeded or failed to do so – the chapter describes the common intellectual foundation that underlay all of them, the political and social philosophy of the **Enlightenment**. The **rationalist** thinkers of this movement, such as **John Locke**, the French *Philosophes*, and **Adam Smith**, all believed that human society was governed by **natural laws**, which could be discovered and fully understood through the application of human reason and the acquisition of knowledge. Progress, prosperity, freedom: all were possible through enlightenment. In some respects, they advocated the application of the "scientific method" to social and political problems and, as the text points out, the Enlightenment and the **Scientific Revolution** of the same period were closely intertwined.

The chapter concludes with a somewhat critical view of the shortcomings of the American Revolution, and a closer examination of two <u>other</u> American revolutions which derived their inspiration (and, partly, their opportunities) from the American and French examples. These are the slave revolt in the French colony of Saint-Domingue, which resulted in the creation of the independent nation of **Haiti**, and the Latin American revolutions of the period, c. 1810-1830, in which the **creole elites** in the American colonies of Spain and Portugal threw off European rule.

CHAPTER OUTLINE

A. Political Revolution: Introduction, Definition and Common Characteristics

B. England's Glorious Revolution, 1688
  1. Philosophical rationales
  2. Hobbes and the "State of Nature"
  3. The Bill of Rights, 1689
  4. John Locke and the Enlightenment
  5. Government by property owners

C. The *Philosophes* and the Enlightenment in the 18th Century
  1. The *Philosophes* and their ideas
  2. Adam Smith and the "Invisible Hand"
  3. The Scientific Revolution

D. Revolution in North America
  1. Causes of the American Revolution
  2. The Constitution and the Bill of Rights, 1789-1791
  3. The first anti-imperial revolution

E. The French Revolution and Napoleon, 1789-1812
  1. Origins of revolution
  2. Historiography of the French Revolution
  3. The revolt of the poor
  4. International war, the "Second Revolution" and the "Reign of Terror," 1791-1799
  5. Napoleon in power, 1799-1812
  6. The Napoleonic Wars and the spread of revolution, 1799-1812

F. Haiti: Slave Revolution and Response, 1791
  1. Toussaint L'Ouverture and the Haitian Revolt
  2. Abolition of slavery and the slave trade: historians debate the causes

G. The End of Colonialism in Latin America: Independence and Disillusionment, 1810-1830
  1. Revolts of the creole elites
  2. Mexico
  3. Brazil
  4. Paraguay: the new historiography
  5. After independence
  6. Religious and economic issues: neo-colonialism and economic dependence

IDENTIFICATION TERMS

For each term provide an identification or definition, an approximate date, a geographical location (if relevant) and – most important – a concise explanation of its importance in the context of the chapter. (Page numbers from the text are provided for your reference.)

Third Estate (p. 478):

Montesquieu (p. 469):

Stamp Act (p.474):

Committee of Public Safety (p. 482):

Glorious Revolution (p. 466):

Code Napoleon (p. 482):

Toussaint L'Ouverture (p. 486):

Encyclopedia (p.470):

creole elites (pp. 489-491):

Leviathan (pp. 463-466):

MULTIPLE CHOICE QUESTIONS

Select the response that completes the sentence or answers the questions best.

1. The American *Declaration of Independence* cited a list of grievances against King George III and Parliament and:
   a. established a federal system of government for the United States
   b. established universal manhood suffrage in the United States
   c. guaranteed to Americans the basic rights enjoyed by the British at the time
   d. declared the social contract between the colonies and England to have been broken

2. The term neocolonialism, in reference to the independent states of Latin America, refers to:
   a. the establishment of control over Latin American economies by Great Britain
   b. the retention of Cuba and Puerto Rico by Spain
   c. the establishment of a Portuguese prince as the Emperor of Brazil
   d. the rise of *caudillos*, or military dictators, in many Latin American nations

3. According to John Locke, "the chief and great end" of government was:
   a. the protection of freedom of religion
   b. the establishment of democracy
   c. the protection of property
   d. the enforcement of the royal will

4. Which of the following has been cited as the main motivation for the abolition of the slave trade, and then of slavery, in the 19th century?
   a. the economic non-profitability of slave agriculture
   b. the fear of further slave revolts, such as occurred in Haiti
   c. humanitarian and rationalist critiques
   d. all of the above

5. The "Second Revolution" phase of the French Revolution began with:
   a. the "Reign of Terror"
   b. the end of the "Reign of Terror"
   c. the attempted escape of Louis XVI and the outbreak of war
   d. the appointment of Napoleon Bonaparte as First Consul

6. The French *philosophe* Voltaire argued in favor of what form of government?
   a. divine-right monarchy
   b. absolute rule by "enlightened despots"
   c. rule by a propertied elite, on the English model
   d. a democracy, governed by the "General Will"

7. In political revolutions, the second phase of the revolution is often more radical and violent than the first, because:
   a. all revolutionaries are violent by nature
   b. once the "social contract" has been broken, society descends into a state of war "of every man against every man"
   c. other governments take advantage of the weakness of revolutionary states and attack them
   d. the groups who united to overthrow the previous system begin to pursue conflicting goals

8. Which of the following policies of the French Revolutionary government was reversed most dramatically by Napoleon Bonaparte?
    a. the emancipation of slaves in France's American colonies
    b. the policy of "careers open to talent" in the French bureaucracy
    c. the toleration of the Protestant and Jewish religions in France
    d. the principle of equality before the law

9. Which of the following people in Latin America did <u>not</u> benefit very much from their nations' independence?
    a. *mazombos*
    b. *mestizos*
    c. *caudillos*
    d. creoles

10. England's "Glorious Revolution" of 1688 was called "glorious" because it was virtually bloodless, compared to the earlier Civil War of the 1640s. It may be truly termed a "revolution" because:
    a. it finally settled the religious and political issues that had troubled England for so long
    b. it overthrew the English monarchy and established a republic under Oliver Cromwell
    c. it put constitutional limits on the powers of the monarchy
    d. it established democratic government in England

11. Which of the following statements best describes the beliefs of the *philosophes?*
    a. Almost all of them were atheists.
    b. Almost all of them were firm believers in democracy.
    c. Almost all of them believed in progress through knowledge.
    d. Almost all of them were revolutionaries.

12. The American "Bill of Rights" of 1791 differed from the English "Bill of Rights" of 1689 in that:
    a. it established freedom of religion and separation of church and state
    b. it established a federal system of government
    c. it removed property requirements for voting
    d. all of the above

13. The term *bourgeoisie* referred to member of which social groups in France?
    a. the nobility and clergy
    b. the urban professional and merchant classes
    c. the rural peasantry
    d. the urban artisans and working classes

14. The "Reign of Terror" was brought to an end in France after:
    a. the end of the "Great Fear"
    b. French armies began to win the war against Austria and Prussia
    c. Napoleon Bonaparte came to power
    d. the national military draft was repealed

15. Which of the following was <u>not</u> a major cause of the downfall of Napoleon?
    a. European nationalism and resentment against French rule
    b. over-extension of French power and the invasion of Russia
    c. revolts against Napoleons' rule in France itself
    d. the naval and commercial power of Great Britain

STUDY QUESTIONS

Consider each of the following questions carefully. Be prepared to supply specific evidence and examples to support your points in a class discussion or concise, well-organized written essay.

1. Why was the European "Scientific Revolution" of the period c. 1500-1750 <u>revolutionary</u>? In what respects did it represent a "fundamental change" in European thought? What were its basic principles and assumptions? How might it be viewed as a precursor to the Enlightenment?

2. In 1776, the signers of the American *Declaration of Independence* believed themselves to be defending "the rights of Englishmen" – as confirmed by the "Glorious Revolution" – against the arbitrary actions of King George III and the British Parliament yet, as the text notes, the American revolution was to prove far more radical than the English Revolution of 1688 had been. Why was this the case?

3. The French Revolution began as a movement to establish a constitutional monarchy on the model of the English Revolution of 1688, but ultimately became even more radical and violent than the American Revolution. Why did this happen? What factors might account for the progressive radicalization of the French Revolution between 1789 and 1794, culminating in the virtual dictatorship of Robespierre's Committee of Public Safety and the "Reign of Terror"?

4. Napoleon Bonaparte is one of the most controversial figures in European history. When in power, he claimed to be consolidating, preserving and even expanding the policies and benefits of the French Revolution. Many of his contemporaries, however, as well as many subsequent observers, believed that many of his actions betrayed the principles of the revolution. A number of modern historians have called him a military dictator, or even an "Enlightened Despot." Whose Napoleon represents the real Napoleon? Cite specific examples and evidence to support your case.

5. It been argued that, even though the various Latin American revolutions resulted in the independence of the Spanish, Portuguese and French colonies and the establishment of republics on the model of the United States, in many respects those upheavals were the least revolutionary revolutions of the period. Would you agree or disagree with this assessment, based on the information presented in the text? To the extent that the argument is a valid one, might there have been any exceptions to the general rule?

6. Examine and assess the opposing explanations concerning the abolition of the slave trade and slavery itself during the period, c. 1770-1870. Considering the examples of the fate of slavery in various places, such as Haiti, the United States, Brazil and the British Empire, which historical explanation(s) seem(s) the most plausible?

HOW DO WE KNOW?

The following questions are based on the various illustrations or quotations and extracts from primary source documents and historical interpretations in the chapter.

1. Both Thomas Hobbes and John Locke based their theories of government on a "social contract." What exactly was the nature of this contract, according to each writer? Who were the parties to the contract, as it were? What was the primary purpose of the contract? In what important respects did their respective views differ?

2. According to the text, the philosophy of the Enlightenment "helped to inspire both the American and the French revolutions" (p. 469). Demonstrate the validity of this argument by comparing principal elements of Enlightenment thought with specific ideas expressed in the American *Declaration of Independence* and French *Declaration of the Rights of Man and the Citizen* and with specific laws or policies which were implemented as a result of each revolution.

3. One of the most influential interpretations of the revolutionary period, c. 1688-1850, that of the American historian R. R. Palmer, views the era as the "Age of the Democratic Revolution". Other commentators, however, have seen the various revolutionary movements more in terms of social class; as revolutions by and for men of property in pursuit of their own economic and political interests. Based on <u>both</u> the historical narrative in the text and any relevant <u>primary source</u> materials in the chapter, which view appears more accurate?

4. In the "Spotlight" section entitled "Francisco Goya: Revolutionary Reality and Rhetoric," the text provides an excellent interpretation of the political uses of art during the revolutionary period. Write a similar commentary for the other famous paintings or prints from the revolutionary period reproduced in the chapter: for example, John Trumbull's group portrait of the *Signing of the Declaration of Independence*; Jacques-Louis David's *Oath of the Tennis Court* and *Napoleon Crossing the Alps*; the anonymous portrait of Simon Bolivar; and the French prints of the women's march on Versailles and the Haitian leader Toussaint L'Ouverture. What images and ideas are the works meant to convey? How are those messages illustrated by the poses and expressions of the figures? By their clothing and accessories?

MAP ANALYSIS

The following exercises are based on the maps on pp. 475, 484, 485 and 488.

1. On the map above, locate and identify the following:
   a. the boundaries of Mexico (1821-1846) and after 1848
   b. the approximate boundaries of the other Latin American republics; the dates of their independence; and the names of their respective former European owners
   c. the major remaining European colonies in the Americas, and identity of their colonial owners
   d. the boundaries of the United States of America in 1783
   e. the major territorial acquisitions of the U.S.A, 1803-1853; and the names of the countries from whom they were acquired
   f. the "Indian Territory" of the United States

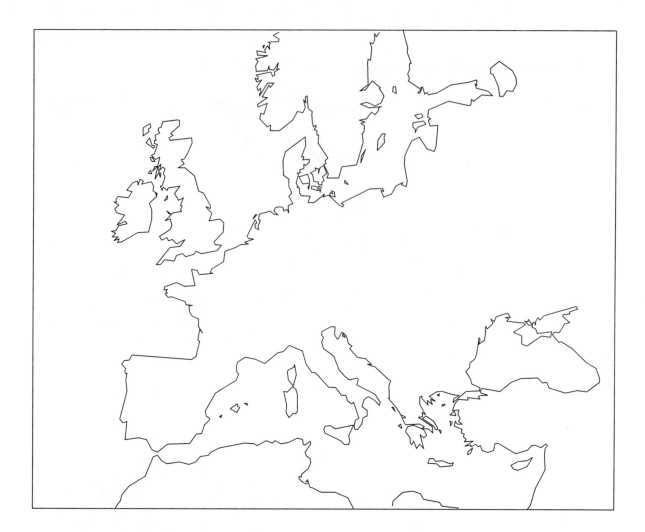

2. On the map above, locate and label the following:
   a. the territory of the French Empire, c. 1812
   b. other states ruled by members of Napoleon's family
   c. the major enemies of the French Empire
   d. <u>underline</u> the name of a country which rebelled against French rule

3. What evidence from the two maps could be cited to support the argument in the text that both France and the United States may have violated some of their own revolutionary principles?

MULTIPLE CHOICE ANSWER KEY (with page references)

1.	D	(474)	6.	B	(471)	11.	C	(470)
2.	A	(495)	7.	D	(462)	12.	A	(474)
3.	B	(462)	8.	A	(486)	13.	B	(478)
4.	D	(487-488)	9.	B	(489-490)	14.	B	(482)
5.	C	(481)	10.	C	(466)	15.	C	(485)

16 THE INDUSTRIAL REVOLUTION
1740 – 1914

THE GLOBAL CONSEQUENCES OF
INDUSTRIAL EXPANSION AND IMPERIALISM

COMMENTARY

As we saw in the previous chapter, the political revolutions in Britain's North American colonies and in France, the most populous and powerful European monarchy at the time, ignited a series of revolutionary movements in Europe, Haiti and Latin America and initiated profound and seemingly irreversible effects on western society. It was not just that the personnel and forms of governments were altered; the entire basis of government was altered, and with it conceptions of society, including those of nationality, social class, human rights, and gender roles. These revolutionary political and social trends continued and grew in the 19th century, manifesting themselves in **democratic** and **nationalist** movements and uprisings against arbitrary or foreign rule throughout Europe, in the transatlantic campaign for the abolition of slavery and the slave trade, and in the smaller, but steadily rising, chorus demanding equal rights for women. This revolutionary dynamic was reinforced by, and eventually merged with another wave of changes brought about by an **Industrial Revolution**, resulting in a tidal wave of political, economic and social change that was to sweep across the entire globe before the end of the century. Just as the political revolutions replaced feudal rulers with elected leaders and established new forms of government, the Industrial Revolution saw the substitution of machines and **inanimate sources of power** for much human labor, the replacement of craft guilds and domestic production by the **factory system** of manufacturing, and the organization of businesses into **corporations** or **cartels**. And, as the political revolutions had resulted in an ever-growing number of citizens participating in government, these technological and organizational changes effected an enormous increase in production and hitherto undreamed of economic growth in the industrialized societies.

The unanticipated consequences of this unprecedented rise in productivity and prosperity were enormous. As the Industrial Revolution spread rapidly from its birthplace in Britain to France, Belgium, Germany, and the United States, new manufacturing cities arose, inhabited by an new form of unskilled urban labor, the industrial **proletariat**, and a new, managerial, middle class. Rapid, unplanned **urbanization** and rampant exploitation of their workers (many of whom were women and young children) by the factory owners led to calls for government intervention and regulation and, as those pleas were heeded in the form of **Factory Acts**, **Poor Laws**, and **Public Health Boards**, large increases in the size, scope, and cost of government. As men of the business and professional classes gained the right to vote, workers began to demand the right to vote and to organize into **labor unions** to protect their interests. Strong resistance to the workers' demands by their employers and their governments led to the rise of **socialist movements**, some of which, following the reasoning of **Karl Marx**, in the *Communist Manifesto*, argued that a revolutionary overthrow of the entire **capitalist** system was the only means by which an equitable distribution of the benefits of industrialization would be achieved. By end of the century, the newly-unified nation of **Germany** and newly reunified (after the Civil War) United States of America had begun to overtake Britain as industrial powers. At the same time, industrialization provided Europeans and Americans with the financial, organizational and technological resources – as well as the motivation – to expand their power and influence throughout the world in the pursuit of new markets for their products, cheap sources or raw materials, new opportunities for capital investments, and new agricultural lands for their ever-growing populations. Millions of Europeans migrated to the Americas, Australia and New Zealand, and parts of Africa and Asia. The non-industrial societies of the world were usually unable to resist the economic encroachment, military domination, and political **colonization** of the "New Imperialism." North America, India, Southeast Asia, and virtually all of Africa came under European or U.S. control by 1900 and Latin America became an economic dependency of the industrial powers. The Ottoman Empire and the Qing Dynasty in China were fatally weakened by their failure to respond to external pressures and the political and social unrest they produced within their borders. Only **Japan** was able to respond effectively, by initiating her own program of industrialization and modernization (as we shall see in the next chapter).

Chapter 16 examines these developments and addresses a number of significant questions. How and why did the Industrial Revolution begin in Britain? How was the second phase of industrialization qualitatively different from the first and why did Britain lose its industrial hegemony to Germany and the United States by 1914? What prevented the proletarian revolutions predicted for the industrialized societies by Marx and Engels? What was the principal motivation for the "New Imperialism"? And how did Europeans and Americans reconcile their often brutal imperial domination of Africans, Asians, and the indigenous peoples of the Americas and the Antipodes with their own, self-proclaimed, beliefs in democracy, human dignity, and the rights of the individual?

CHAPTER OUTLINE

A. The Industrial Revolution: <u>What was it?</u> <u>What was its significance?</u>

B. Britain, 1740-1860
    1. Revolution in textile manufacture
    2. Capital goods: iron, steam engines, railways and steamships
    3. Why did the Industrial Revolution begin in Britain? <u>How do we know?</u>

C. The Second Stage of Industrialization, 1860-1910
    1. New products and new nations
        a. steel and chemical industries
        b. electricity
    2. Factory production
    3. Warfare and industrialization
    4. Effects of the "Second Industrial Revolution" worldwide

D. Social Changes: the Conditions of Working People
    1. <u>What do we know and how do we know it?</u>
    2. Demographic causes and effects of the Industrial Revolution
    3. Winners and losers in the Industrial Revolution
        a. social and economic effects on the workers
        b. public health legislation

E. Political Reaction in Britain and Europe, 1800-1914
    1. Political responses in Britain
        a. the Reform Acts of 1832 and 1867
        b. Factory Acts and Chartism
        c. labor organization and Parliament
    2. Labor organization in Britain
    3. Labor organization outside Britain
        a. Karl Marx and theories of worker revolution
        b. Germany, 1870-1914
        c. the United States, 1870-1914
        d. France, 1870-1914

F. Competition among Industrial Powers: the Quest for Empire
    1. European pre-eminence and "social Darwinism"
    2. The Ottoman Empire: the "Sick Man of Europe," 1829-1876
    3. Southeast Asia and Indonesia, 1795-1880
    4. India, 1858-1914
    5. China, 1800-1914
        a. the Opium Wars and the Taiping Rebellion, 1839-1864
        b. the Boxer Rebellion, 1898-1900

G. Africa, 1653-1912
    1. Egypt, 1798-1882
    2. Algeria, 1830-1871
    3. South Africa, 1652-1910
        a. Zulus, Boers and British, 1816-1902
        b. Labor issues: coercion and unionization
    4. European explorers in central Africa
    5. The "scramble for Africa," 1884-1912

H. Motives for European Colonization: Differing Historical Interpretations

IDENTIFICATION TERMS

For each term provide an identification or definition, an approximate date, a geographical location (if relevant) and – most important – a concise explanation of its significance in the context of the chapter. (Page numbers from the text are provided for your reference.

Luddite riots (p.501):

Natives Land Act (p. 531):

Hiram Maxim (p. 510):

Opium War (pp. 527-528):

Edwin Chadwick (p. 513):

Otto von Bismarck (pp. 517-518):

cartels (p. 507):

Chartist Movement (p. 514):

The Mahdi (p. 533):

Friedrich Engels (p.512):

MULTIPLE CHOICE QUESTIONS

Select the response that completes the sentence or answers the question best.

1. Which of the following would be the best description of Karl Marx's attitude toward European colonialism?
    a. Marx opposed colonialism, arguing that peoples in Africa and Asia should be left to themselves.
    b. Marx supported colonialism, because he shared the belief that European society was superior to all others.
    c. Marx deplored colonial exploitation, but advocated the introduction of capitalism as a way to promote socialism.
    d. Marx deplored colonialism and the introduction of capitalism, but argued they were still an improvement over the peoples' previous conditions.

2. The series of improvements in the spinning of cotton thread, at the beginning of the Industrial Revolution in England, was necessitated by:
    a. the decline of the woolen industry
    b. improvements in the weaving process
    c. competition from imported cotton textiles from India
    d. the invention of the steam engine

3. The Reform Act of 1832 in Britain:
    a. forbade the employment of children under the age of nine in textile mills
    b. repealed the Corn Laws, quotas on the importation of grain
    c. gave workers the right to strike
    d. gave the right to vote to professionals and businessmen

4. Which of the following product of the early Industrial Revolution would <u>not</u> be classified as "capital goods"?
    a. steam engines
    b. iron bars
    c. railway cars
    d. cotton cloth

5. India became a "model colony" of Britain in the later 19th century, because:
    a. it imported British textile and investment capital, while exporting raw materials
    b. it experienced no major revolts after 1858
    c. it began its own industrial revolution, producing textile and steel
    d. its educational system was modeled on Britain's

6. Which of the following is the most accurate description of the main cause of the Boer War of 1899-1902?
   a. British attempts to protect the native African population from Boer attacks
   b. competition for the mineral wealth of the Boer Republics in South Africa
   c. British efforts to protect the Boer farmers from Zulu attacks
   d. Boer encroachment on British colonies in South Africa

7. The new technologies, organizational innovations and production of consumer goods that characterized the "Second Industrial Revolution" were exploited most effectively in Germany and:
   a. France
   b. Britain
   c. the United States
   d. Russia

8. Karl Marx and Friedrich Engels prophesied the end of the perpetual class struggle through:
   a. a progressive income tax, free education, and the abolition of child labor
   b. violent revolution and the abolition of private property
   c. the legalization of trade unions and workers' right to strike
   d. giving the proletariat (working classes) the right to vote

9. In terms of cost in human lives, the largest war of the 19th century was:
   a. the Crimean War
   b. the Taiping Rebellion
   c. the American Civil War
   d. the Opium War

10. The argument that "those who were strong deserved their superiority, and those who were weak deserved their inferiority" was a basic assumption of the philosophy of:
   a. social Darwinism
   b. Marxism
   c. neocolonialism
   d. capitalism

11. Karl Marx's predictions of an imminent proletarian revolution in his *Communist Manifesto* did not come to pass in industrialized societies such as Britain and Germany because:
   a. workers won the right to vote and formed their own political parties
   b. labor unions were legalized and won the right to strike
   c. the British and German governments enacted laws to improve working conditions and provide accident insurance for workers
   d. all of the above

12. Which of the following was not an immediate effect of the Opium Wars?
   a. the expansion of the opium trade in China
   b. the Boxer Rebellion
   c. British acquisition of Hong Kong
   d. the granting of immunity from Chinese laws to European merchants

13. The principal demands of the Chartist Movement in Britain included:
   a. repeal of the Corn Laws
   b. free public education
   c. universal manhood suffrage
   d. all of the above

14. According to the text, the "Scramble for Africa" effectively began with:
    a. the discovery of gold in South Africa
    b. the building of the Suez Canal
    c. Belgian annexation of the Congo
    d. the Berlin Conference of 1884

15. Which of the following non-European states also engaged in imperial expansion during the 19ᵗʰ century?
    a. Egypt
    b. the Zulu kingdom
    c. Japan
    d. all of the above

STUDY QUESTIONS

Consider each of the following questions carefully. Be prepared to supply specific evidence and examples to support your points in a class discussion or concise, well-organized written essay.

1. Why did the Industrial Revolution begin in Britain when it did? What specific factors have been identified as being crucial in laying the groundwork for industrialization and <u>how</u> did they do so?

2. What made the "Second Industrial Revolution" different from the first? Why do you suppose that it was Germany and the United States, rather than Britain, who took the lead in the second phase of industrialization?

3. Explain the effects of European encroachment on the Ottoman Empire, China, and India in the 19th century. How did these societies attempt to respond to the challenge of the industrialization? What factors affected their responses?

4. The Industrial Revolution in Britain and elsewhere was promoted primarily by men who were firm believers in capitalism, free market enterprise, and *laissez-faire*. Yet one of the most significant results of industrialization in Europe and the United States was the growth of government and increased government intervention in business and society. How can this apparent contradiction be explained?

HOW DO WE KNOW?

The following questions are based on the various illustrations or quotations and extracts from primary source documents and historical interpretations in the text.

1. According to their *Communist Manifesto* (1848), why did Karl Marx and Friedrich Engels believe that the only recourse of the industrial proletariat was violent revolution? Why did this prediction turn out to be incorrect in Britain, Germany and the United States, the most industrialized societies at the end of the 19th century?

2. Discuss the various historical interpretations of the motivations and effects of the "New Imperialism" as reviewed on pp. 535-536. What was the primary goal of the imperial powers? What effects did imperialism have on the subject peoples and their societies?

3. What exactly was "The White Man's Burden" according to Rudyard Kipling? What political ideas and arguments were employed by Europeans and Americans to justify imperialism?

4. What were the direct effects of industrialization and urbanization on the working classes? What types of evidence do we have for these effects? How did industrial workers respond to the new conditions? What different methods did they utilize to improve their circumstances?

MAP ANALYSIS

The following exercises are based on the maps on pp. 520, 528 and 532.

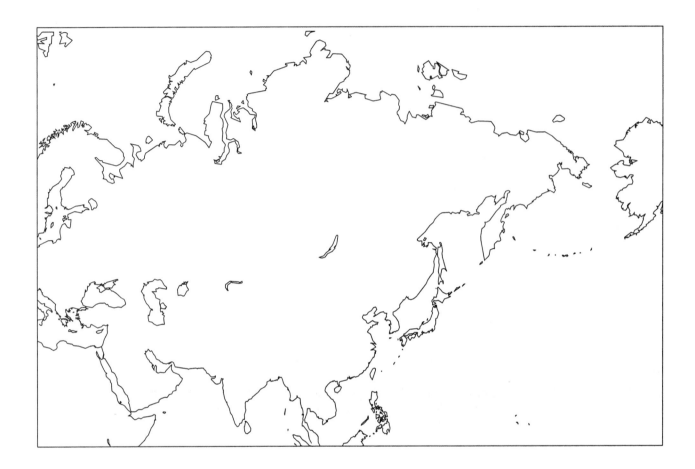

On the maps of Asia above and Africa on the opposite page, locate and identify the following:

1. The territories which became colonies of Britain, France, the United States, Germany, the Netherlands, Russia, Japan, Italy and Belgium; with the dates of annexation.
2. The areas which came under the indirect or economic influence of those countries.
3. The areas which experienced major anti-imperial or anti-colonial revolts; with the names and dates of those rebellions.

MULTIPLE CHOICE ANSWER KEY

1.	C	(535)	6.	B	(531)	11.	D	(passim)
2.	B	(498)	7.	C	(505-510)	12.	A	(529)
3.	D	(514)	8.	B	(517)	13.	C	(514)
4.	D	(501)	9.	B	(529)	14.	D	(521)
5.	A	(525)	10.	A	(521)	15.	D	(passim)

17   SOCIAL REVOLUTIONS
1830 – 1914

URBANIZATION, GENDER RELATIONS, AND NATIONALISM, WEST AND EAST

COMMENTARY

Chapter 17 concludes the textbook's survey of the revolutions which transformed the modern world by examining the global revolutionary changes that occurred in the patterns of urban life, in **gender** relations, and the development of the **nation-state**. As was the case with the gradual evolution of participatory democracy and the growth of the regulatory role of government (see Chapter 16), all three of these movements were, in a sense, products of what the 20th century British historian E. J. Hobsbawm has called the **"Dual Revolution"** – the intertwined and mutually reinforcing effects of the political and industrial revolutions of the 18th and 19th centuries. Urbanization is a perfect example. As Spodek points out, "Cities grew because they served new functions for more people. One of these functions," he continues, "… was the increasing importance of central government" (538). The growth of Paris, London, and Washington, D.C., in the 19th century all demonstrated this. On the other hand, some of the century's most spectacularly rapid urban growth was the result of industrialization. It was factory cities such Manchester and Birmingham in England, Chicago and Pittsburgh in the United States, and Hamburg and Essen in Germany, that were to become the symbols of the age. And, as the chapter explains, industry was not only the lure which attracted millions of migrants to the cities' mills, factories, offices, and food-processing plants; it also provided the technology which enabled cities to expand outward and upward (in the form of subways, electric trolley-lines, and structural steel for the new – 10-story high! – **"skyscrapers"**) and made them safer, more sanitary, and more livable (in the form of sewage treatment systems, gas and electric lighting, and elevators). Similarly, the cumulative effects of the "Dual Revolution" called into question the traditionally subordinate roles and status of women. The emphasis of the American and French Revolutions on political equality and the "Rights of Man" inevitably led to discussion of the rights of women. The wrenching social changes of the Industrial Revolution further transformed gender relations by replacxing the family with the factory as the primary unit of production and by gradually relegating women – even working-class women – to the inferior economic role of non-productive "homemakers." It was this glaring contradiction that gave rise to the **women's movement** with its demands for equal rights in marriage, divorce, and property ownership; equal opportunities in the workplace, and **women's suffrage** ("Votes for Women").

Nationalism and the nation-state were also fostered as much by industrialization as they were by revolutionary political ideas and warfare. The concept of nationhood envisions a people united by common cultural, linguistic and historical bonds, and that of the nation-state sees that people, or **nation**, as constituting basis for the government: "The source of all **sovereignty** [supreme power in the government] is located essentially in the nation," according to the French *Declaration of the Rights of Man and the Citizen* (1789)… However, as Spodek notes, "At least since the French Revolution and the industrial revolution, the nation has been the vehicle for the spread of trade networks and capitalism throughout the world" (556). Economic unity was a critical advantage for Britain during its industrialization, as we saw in the previous chapter, and the same was to be true later for the United States, Germany, and Japan.

The chapter begins with an inquiry into late 19th and early 20th century views of urbanization and its problems and proposals for reform, comparing the new industrial cities of the western world to the commercial and administrative centers, such as Singapore, that Europeans built in the colonies. Changing gender roles are also viewed in a global perspective: Europeans, it seems, imposed their beliefs regarding women's rights on their African and Asian colonies, just as they imposed political rule and economic domination. Finally, the chapter looks at various forms of nationalism, as they manifested themselves in the classical linguistic-cultural nationalism of France and the newly-unified nation-states of Italy and Germany (and Japan); in the concept of a multicultural nation formed around a political ideal, as in the United States; and in the movement for a Jewish ethnic and religious nation, **Zionism**.

CHAPTER OUTLINE

A. Introduction: Political, Industrial and Social Revolutions

B. New Patterns of Urban Life

    1. Government centralization, industrialization, and urbanization
    2. The conditions of urbanization: <u>how do we know</u>?
        a. Primary documents of the times
        b. Poets of the city: Baudelaire and Whitman
    3. "Urban Sprawl" – <u>How do we know</u>?
    4. The non-industrial, non-European city

C. Gender Relations: Their Significance in an Age of Revolution

    1. Gender and history
    2. The movement towards equality
        a. the French revolution and women
            i. Condorcet; Olympe de Gouges
            ii. reaction in the *Code Napoleon*
        c. the 19th century
            i. Mary Wollstonecraft
            ii. the Seneca Falls Convention (1848)
            iii. John Stuart Mill (1869)
        d. the movement for women's suffrage
    3. Gender relationships and the Industrial Revolution
    4. Gender relationships and colonization
    5. Women's bodies and reform: India, China, Europe

D. Nationalism: <u>What Do We Know</u>?

    1. What is nationalism?
    2. French nationalism
    3. Nationalism in the United States
    4. Nationalism on the periphery of western Europe: positive and negative faces of nationalism
    5. The rise of Zionism in Europe
    6. Italy and Germany
        a. Mazzini, Cavour, Garibaldi, and Italian unification (1831-1870)
        b. Bismarck, Prussia, and German unification (1848-1871)
    7. China and Chinese nationalism (1856-1911)
    8. Anti-colonial revolts (1857-1912)

E. Japan: From Isolation to Equality, 1867-1914

    1. The end of the Shogunate
    2. Policies of the Meiji government
    3. Restructuring government
    4. Restructuring the economy
    5. Urbanization
    6. Cultural and Educational change
    7. Gender relations
    8. War, colonialism, and equality in the family of nations
        a. the Sino-Japanese War
        b. the Russo-Japanese War

IDENTIFICATION TERMS

For each term provide an identification or definition, an approximate date, a geographical location (if relevant) and – most important – a concise explanation of its historical significance. (Page numbers are provided for your reference.)

Tsushima Straits (p.569):

"family wage" (p. 551):

Jakob and Wilhelm Grimm (p. 561):

The Subjection of Women (p. 549):

Theodore Herzl (p.558):

Charter Oath of 1868 (p. 563):

Indian National Congress (p. 562)

garden city movement (p. 545):

Young Italy (p. 560):

Emmeline Pankhurst (p. 551):

MULTIPLE CHOICE QUESTIONS

Select the response that completes the sentence or answers the question best.

1. "Gendered" events in history are ones that:
    a. lead to male domination
    b. affect men and women differently
    c. promote feminism
    d. all of the above

2. Nationalism in the United States differed from that of continental Europe in that:
    a. in theory, it was not identified with a specific language or ethnic group
    b. it was imposed by force (during the Civil War)
    c. minority groups, such as native Americans and African slaves, were excluded from the nation
    d. it was not promoted by the government

3. What was the aim of Charles Booth in his research for *Life and Labour of the People in London*?
    a. to investigate the causes and cures for poverty in the midst of wealth
    b. to investigate the reasons for the growth of London in the 19th century
    c. to investigate the causes and remedies for "urban sprawl" in London
    d. to investigate the various occupations and neighborhoods of the people of London

4. The Japanese scholar and politician Sakuma Shozan is most closely associated with which of the following slogans?
    a. "Revere the Emperor; expel the Barbarian!"
    b. "A rich country and a strong military!"
    c. "Knowledge shall be sought throughout the world!"
    d. "Eastern Ethics; Western Science!"

5. Historians now argue that the main reason western reformers sought to abolish Asian practices such as Chinese foot-binding and *sati* in India was:
    a. to gain support for imperial rule from women in Asia
    b. to promote the equality of women and men around the world
    c. to demonstrate their moral superiority
    d. all of the above

6. The cities established by Europeans in their Asian and African colonies differed from those in their European "Mother Countries" in that:
    a. fostered local political fragmentation, rather than national development
    b. restricted economic growth to low levels of production
    c. tended to emphasize administrative functions
    d. all of the above

7. In *The Subjection of Women* (1869), the English economist and philosopher, argued for the equality of women, based on the proposition that:
    a. the subjection of women was akin to slavery
    b. equality of adults was essential to warm emotional ties and rewarding family life
    c. the concept of the "family wage" was economically unsound
    d. all of the above

8. In "What is a Nation" (1882), the French philosopher Ernest Renan asserted his belief that nationalism was replacing _____ as a central concern in people's lives.
    a. economics
    b. democracy
    c. religion
    d. social class

9. The revolutionary social transformation known as the "Meiji Restoration" in Japan was led by:
    a. the emperor
    b. the *shogun*
    c. the *samurai*
    d. the middle-classes

10. In Britain, women finally won the right to vote, as a result of:
    a. the efforts of the Labour Party
    b. women's activities during the First World War
    c. the militant tactics of the suffragettes
    d. the writings of John Stuart Mill

11. A common characteristic of German commentators on urbanization was:
    a. their tendency to view cities and their social effects in a negative light
    b. their emphasis on vigorous neighborhood communities
    c. their opposition to the "garden city" concept
    d. their lack of concern for the poor

12. A common feature of *sati*, foot-binding, and waist-binding among women in India, China, and Europe, respectively was that:
    a. they were all designed to emphasize female dependence on men
    b. they were all restricted to women of the wealthier classes in their respective societies
    c. they were all opposed by European women
    d. they were all successfully abolished in the 19th century

13. The unification of Italy and Germany were similar in that:
    a. both were imposed by force
    b. both led to the political domination of the new country by one particular region
    c. both were opposed by the Habsburg Monarchy in Austria
    d. all of the above

14. The argument that China did not develop its own, unique form of nationalism, the text argues, was based on:
    a. the fact that the Qing Dynasty was not ethnically Chinese
    b. a narrowly eurocentric definition of nationalism
    c. the fact that, unlike Italy and Germany, China was already unified
    d. the failure of revolts such as the Taiping and Boxer Rebellions

15. The event that motivated Theodore Herzl to promote the concept of Zionism was:
    a. the Dreyfus Affair in France
    b. the unification of Germany
    c. persecution of Jews in Russia
    d. the weakening of the Ottoman Empire

Consider each of the following questions carefully. Be prepared to supply specific evidence and examples to support your points in a class discussion or concise, well-organized written essay.

1. Define "nationalism." How can we explain the different forms nationalism assumed in different countries? (Cite specific examples.)

2. Discuss the development of feminism and the movement for women's rights as a product of the "Dual Revolution." In what specific ways did both the French Revolution and subsequent democratic political movements and the Industrial Revolution encourage demands for equal rights for women?

3. Compare the development of nation-states in North America, Italy and Germany during the 19th century. In what respects were these developments similar? How were they different?

4. Why was Japan able to confront western imperialism so successfully and transform its society so quickly, as compared with China? What specific factors may have set Japan apart from other nations in Asia and Africa?

5. What factors and forces obstructed the movement for women's rights in western nations in the period, c. 1790-1914? Why were so many women lukewarm to the idea? What events ultimately helped women toward their goals?

6. Explain the comment in the text that states, "Nationalism has always had two faces." What are the "positive" and "negative" faces of nationalism? Cite specific examples.

HOW DO WE KNOW?

The following questions are based on the various illustrations or quotations and extracts from primary source documents and historical interpretations in the chapter.

1. Compare the specific arguments and general attitudes regarding urbanization of American commentators such as Walt Whitman, Adna Ferrin Weber and the members of the "Chicago School" with those of Europeans such as Charles Baudelaire, Charles Booth, Max Weber and Oswald Spengler. In what respects did they differ? How might one account for those differences?

2. Compare the arguments for women's rights, as put forward by specific French, British, Norwegian, and American women's advocates, c. 1790-1890. In what ways did they reflect specific political, social, religious and economic developments in their own countries?

MAP ANALYSIS

The following exercise is based on the maps on p. 559.

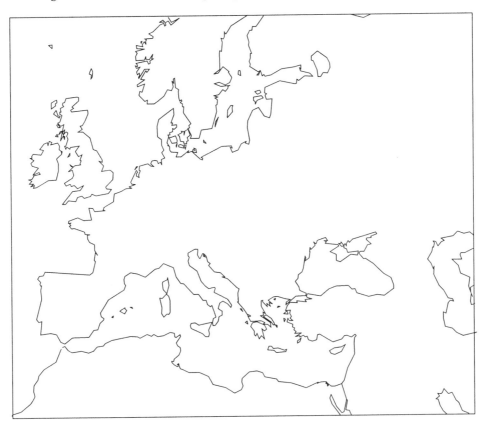

On the map above, locate and label each of the following:
  a. Piedmont, Prussia, Lombardy, Bavaria, Venetia, Bohemia, the Papal States, France, the Kingdom of the Two Sicilies, Alsace-Lorraine, the Austrian Empire, Poland, the Russian Empire
  b. the boundaries of the North German Confederation, the Kingdom of Italy and the German Empire
  c. underline the names of territories which were added to Italy and Germany by war with France or Austria

MULTIPLE CHOICE ANSWER KEY (with page references)

1.	B	(546)	6.	D	(546)	11.	A	(542)
2.	A	(557)	7.	B	(549)	12.	B	(552-553)
3.	A	(541)	8.	C	(556)	13.	D	(559-560)
4.	D	(563)	9.	C	(563)	14.	B	(561)
5.	C	(555)	10.	B	(550)	15.	A	(559)

PART
8

Exploding Technologies

1914 – 1990s

CONTESTED VISIONS
OF A
NEW INTERNATIONAL ORDER

18 TECHNOLOGIES OF MASS-PRODUCTION AND DESTRUCTION

1914 – 1990s

WHAT IS A TECHNOLGICAL SYSTEM AND WHY IS IT IMPORTANT?

COMMENTARY

In many respects, Part Eight – *Exploding Technologies* – may be seen as a continuation of, or perhaps a sequel to, the previous section on revolutionary social change. In terms of technological change, the 20th century, which is surveyed in the last section of the book, has been the most revolutionary era to date. This is true not only with respect to **technologies of mass destruction**, but also for those which have lengthened, enhanced, and improved human life, and, most recently for changes in **information and communications technologies** that have brought the regions of the world closer together and facilitated the dissemination of all forms of knowledge. The six chapters in this section spend much time examining both the opportunities and problems that this technological explosion presented to the world as a whole (Chapter 18) and to certain selected regions, specifically Russia and Japan (Chapter 19), China and Japan (20), the Middle East (21), Africa (22), and Latin America (23). But woven inextricably into this survey are the continuing and inter-related effects of the political and social revolutions that transformed the globe during the 18th and 19th centuries. These too – especially problems emanating from the political philosophies of mass democracy and nationalism and from population growth and migration – reached crisis proportions in the 20th century.

Chapter 18 – "Technologies of Mass-Production and Destruction" – confronts some of the most disastrous (or potentially so) consequences of the technological, political, and social revolutions that have shaped the modern world to date: the global **population explosion**, the cataclysmic **world wars** of the first half of the 20th century, the awesome growth of the power of the modern **nation-state**, the ideological confrontation of the **Cold War** and the specter of a **nuclear war**, and the destructive effects of modern technology on the world's **ecology**. It also examines the ongoing attempts at dealing with those problems through **international organizations**, such as the **League of Nations** (1919-1939), the **United Nations** (1945-   ), and various regional organizations, such as the **European Union**. It also demonstrates the unavoidable – and many times unanticipated – interconnectedness of global change. Both **World War I** and **World War II**, as the text points out, were caused, in part, by the imperialist ambitions of nation-states competing for territory and natural resources to feed their growing populations and fuel their expanding economies. They were facilitated by the ability of governments – through mass education and communication – to mobilize their populations to make enormous sacrifices on behalf of such abstract ideas as "the nation" or "democracy" or the "purity of the race." They encouraged the development of technologies of industrialized mass murder such as the machine gun, poison gas, indiscriminate aerial bombing, atomic weapons and intercontinental ballistic missiles that have caused the deaths of over 100 million people during this century. And they necessitated the creation of the "Leviathan" of the of the 20th century state and the creation of technologies that pose a real threat to the continuance of life on earth. And, in spite of all the century's wars, the world's population has quadrupled since 1900 and is expected to double again within the next twenty-five years – the result, once again, of modern technologies: medical, agricultural and transportation, in this case. The chapter records these problems of 20th century civilization, as well as some of the intellectual discontent and reflection they have produced. But it also demonstrates how the problems of war, overpopulation, impersonal state structures, and environmental dangers have promoted attempts at regional and global international cooperation in dealing with the "fallout" from modern technology and converting it to the betterment of human society.

CHAPTER OUTLINE

A. Technological Systems

    1. Technology and technological systems: definitions
    2. Technological transformations in the 20th century
        a. demographic shifts and population increase
        b. urbanization and migration
        c. domestic change
        d. energy
        e. warfare

B. World War

    1. World War I: 1914-1918
        a. origins of the war
        b. trench warfare on the "Western Front"
        c. the United States enters the war
        d. new weapons: machine guns, tanks, poison gas
    2. The Treaty of Versailles: 1919
        a. end of the Habsburg and Ottoman Empires
        b. Germany: war guilt and reparations
        c. the League of Nations
    3. Economic depression and the expansion of the welfare state between the wars
        a. causes of the depression
        b. economic and political effects in Britain, the U.S.A. and Germany
    4. World War II: 1939-1945
        a. origins of the war
            i. Hitler and the Nazis in Germany
            ii. Mussolini and Italian Fascism
            iii. Japan and China
        b. the war in Europe and Asia
        c. technology in the war
            i. war production
            ii. the mobilization of women
        d. the horrors of war
            i. the Holocaust
            ii. the atomic bombs

C. The Leviathan State

    1. The military state
    2. The "military-industrial complex"

D. The Image of Humanity

    1. Gandhi on technology and "civilization"
    2. Picasso, Freud, and Yeats
    3. Elie Wiesel

E. International and National Institutional Planning: 1945-1990's

    1. The Cold War: 1945-91
    2. The United Nations today
    3. Ecological issues

F. The Nation-State, International Organization, and the Individual

IDENTIFICATION TERMS

For each term provide an identification or definition, an approximate date, a geographical location (if relevant) and – most important – a concise explanation of its significance in the context of the chapter. (Page numbers from the text are provided for your reference.)

UNICEF (p. 601):

Total War (p. 591):

Elie Wiesel (p. 597):

"Green Revolution" (p. 577):

European Union (EU) (p. 606):

Fascism (p. 589):

Silent Spring (p.604):

Franklin D. Roosevelt (p. 586):

Triple Alliance (p. 582):

Hiroshima (pp. 593-94; 600):

MULTIPLE CHOICE QUESTIONS

Select the response that completes the sentence or answers the question best.

1. Demographers have suggested that the best way to reduce population growth in poorer countries is to:
    a. enact strict government population control and family-planning policies
    b. implement voluntary sterilization programs
    c. improve health conditions to assure parents that their babies will live to adulthood
    d. reduce food supplies and let nature take its course

2. The immediate cause of the outbreak of the First World War was:
    a. the rivalry between the Triple Alliance and the Triple Entente
    b. competition among nations over colonies and markets
    c. the cynical manipulation of nationalist feelings by producers of new weapons
    d. the assassination of the Austrian Archduke by a Serbian terrorist group

3. The event which precipitated U.S. entry into the war was:
    a. Germany's invasion of Belgium in 1914
    b. Germany's submarine attacks on unarmed merchant ships in 1917
    c. Russia's collapse and withdrawal from the war in 1917-1918
    d. Germany's use of poison gas in 1915

4. Which of the following was not a provision of the Treaty of Versailles?
    a. the disarmament of Germany
    b. the independence of Germany's former African and Asian colonies
    c. the dissolution of the Habsburg Empire and independence of Poland, Hungary and Czechoslovakia
    d. the imposition of financial reparations on Germany

5. Which of the following was a major cause of the Great Depression?
    a. the imposition of financial reparations on Germany
    b. the return of millions of soldiers to the European workforce after the war
    c. the destruction caused by the war in Europe
    d. agricultural overproduction and surpluses

6. Which of the following was a major result of the Great Depression?
    a. political unrest and a loss of faith in democratic government in Europe
    b. the enactment of massive government public works programs
    c. Nazi electoral success in Germany
    d. all of the above

7. During the Spanish Civil War, nationalist rebel forces fighting against the democratically-elected government received considerable military aid from:
    a. Germany and Italy
    b. Britain and France
    c. the Soviet Union
    d. the United States

8. During World War II, women were <u>not</u> recruited into the work force in large numbers in:
   a. Britain
   b. Germany
   c. the Soviet Union
   d. the United States

9. Jews were targeted for destruction by the Nazis primarily for _____ reasons in the Holocaust.
   a. racial
   b. economic
   c. religious
   d. political

10. When President Dwight Eisenhower left office in 1960, he warned the American people about the dangers of:
    a. Soviet communism
    b. nuclear war
    c. the military-industrial complex
    d. all of the above

11. The Marshall Plan was initiated by the United States to help Western Europe recover from:
    a. World War I
    b. the Great Depression
    c. World War II
    d. the Cold War

12. Which of the following is <u>not</u> an agency of the United Nations?
    a. UNESCO
    b. WHO
    c. the World Bank
    d. OPEC

13. The "greenhouse effect" is another name for which of the following ecological problems?
    a. global warming
    b. deforestation
    c. acid rain
    d. depletion of the ozone layer

14. A major problem, inhibiting the United Nations from acting more effectively in the areas of international peacekeeping, global environmental issues, and related matters, has been:
    a. disagreements between developed and developing member nations
    b. Cold War rivalries between the U.S. and the Soviet Union and their allies
    c. the absence of sovereign power and necessity for voluntary compliance and cooperation
    d. all of the above

15. The most successful movement towards international cooperation and regional integration since 1945 has been undertaken by which of the following organizations?
    a. the Organization of American States (OAS)
    b. the European Union (EU)
    c. the Association of South East Asian Nations (ASEAN)
    d. the Organization of African Unity (OAU)

STUDY QUESTIONS

Consider each of the following questions carefully. Be prepared to supply specific evidence and examples to support your points in a class discussion or concise, well-organized written essay.

1. Although millions of people have died as the result of 20th century wars, the world's population has grown enormously, especially in the so-called "Third World." Explain the factors contributing to this increase; the reasons why governments' attempts to limit population growth have often been unsuccessful, and the measures that demographers have suggested to remedy the situation.

2. Discuss the responsibilities, accomplishments, and problems of the United Nations. How successful have its various agencies been in dealing with issues of international peacekeeping, economic development, and health and environmental issues? What factors have hindered its performance? Should the United States continue to support the United Nations?

3. The previous chapter (p. 558) referred to the "two faces" of nationalism. Discuss the specific examples of the "negative" face of nationalism that were described in the present chapter. How did nationalism contribute to the causes of the two world wars? To problems facing the world since 1945?

4. Some historians have argued that the First (1914-1918) and Second (1939-1945) World Wars were simply two stages of the same global conflict, separated by a "twenty-year truce." How valid is that argument? Considering the issues that precipitated each war, in what respects were they part of the same struggle? In what way might World War I be seen as the major cause of World War II?

5. The two world wars brought about a number of cumulative changes in the governments and societies of their major participants. What were the most important of these changes, according to the text? How, exactly, were these changes a result of the wars?

HOW DO WE KNOW?

The following questions are based on the various illustrations or quotations and extracts from primary source documents and historical interpretations in the chapter.

1. Why is Rachel Carson's *Silent Spring* regarded as one of the most important books of the 20th century? How did it call attention to global environmental issues? What are the most pressing ecological issues facing the world at this time?

2. Some of the century's most noted figures have leveled a blistering critique of the concepts of "civilization" and "progress" in light of the uses and misuses of technology since 1914. With specific reference to the works of Mohandas Gandhi, Sigmund Freud, William Butler Yeats, Elie Wiesel, Pablo Picasso, and Albert Camus (pp. 596-601), discuss the main points of this critique.

3. Considering the photograph and eyewitness testimony of the atomic bombing of Hiroshima in 1945 (p. 600), was the use of atomic weapons on Japan by the United States in World War II justified? What arguments have been put forward in defense of this action? What criticisms have been made by subsequent commentators? Was the killing of several million defenseless civilians by aerial bombing in World War II in any way comparable to the Nazis' destruction of several million defenseless Jews, as some historians have argued?

MAP ANALYSIS

The exercise below is based on the maps on pp. 584, 587, and 590.

On the map above, locate and identify the following:
  a. the European "Allies" and "Central Powers" in World War I
  b. the new countries that were created in Europe after World War I
  c. the respective enemy coalitions in Europe during World War II
  d. the major areas of fighting and at least six major battles in each war

MULTIPLE CHOICE ANSWER KEY (with page references)

1.	C	(528)	6.	D	(588-589)	11.	C	(602)
2.	D	(583)	7.	A	(589)	12.	D	(603)
3.	B	(584)	8.	B	(592)	13.	A	(605)
4.	B	(585-586)	9.	A	(592)	14.	D	(606)
5.	D	(587)	10.	C	(595)	15.	B	(606)

19   THE SOVIET UNION AND JAPAN
1914 – 1997

PLAYING TECHNOLOGICAL
CATCH-UP WITH THE WEST

COMMENTARY

Chapter 19 compares the different paths to technological power, economic development, and social and political modernization followed by two of the great powers of the late 20th century, Russia and Japan. As the author points out in the chapter introduction, the two countries were radically different from one another in many ways. Russia, at the beginning of the century, was huge: the largest country in the world in total land area. It was rich in natural resources. It had a long, albeit turbulent, history of connections – cultural, religious, economic, and military – with the great powers of Europe, and since the reign of Czar **Peter the Great**, had been counted as one of them. Its population was ethnically and religiously diverse, including Finns, Balts, Armenians, Turkic peoples and Tatars (Mongols), along with numerous Slavic groups besides the majority "Great Russians," inside its borders, which had been steadily expanded since Peter's time. Japan, on the other hand was small, and located on the periphery of east Asia. It had virtually no natural resources: even agricultural land was in short supply in an archipelago that was mostly volcanic mountains. Although not totally cut off from the rest of Asia and the world, its **Tokugawa shoguns** had maintained a highly effective policy of isolation since the early 17th century. Ethnically and culturally, it was one of the most homogeneous societies on earth. At the same time, however, there were some striking similarities. Both countries had developed relatively sophisticated and effective government bureaucracies, based on the Russian nobility and the Japanese **samurai.** Both had large labor pools of rural peasants; while on the other hand both had a number of provincial commercial centers. And both nations were shocked out of their technological backwardness at exactly the same time, between 1853 and 1856, when Russia was defeated in the **Crimean War** by Britain and France and Japan was forced to open its harbors to western trade and cultural influence by the power of the United States Navy. Thus, both countries began playing "catch-up" at the same time and for the same reasons.

The interesting pattern of similarity and contrasts continued into the 20th century, as well. Both Czarist Russia and **Meiji** Japan embarked on the path of technological transformation through programs of government directed capitalism and the importation of large quantities of foreign capital and expertise. Both sought to expand their trade and influence at China's expense, which led to the **Russo-Japanese War** (1904 – 05)and a humiliating defeat for Russia.
World War I proved a turning point for both countries, but in very different ways. Japan benefited economically, as the war spurred industrial production and resulted in the acquisition of many of Germany's Pacific outposts. And with Europe and the United States otherwise occupied, more inroads were made on the Asian mainland. For Russia, the war brought government collapse and the **Bolshevik Revolution.** Promising "Peace, bread, and land," **Lenin** and his bolsheviks seized power in 1917 and, under Lenin's successor, **Josef Stalin**, imposed a system of forced agricultural **collectivization**, centralized economic planning, and rapid, state-run industrialization that was to modernize Russia overnight; help the nation survive German invasion and the loss of 20 million people in World War II; and transform the country into a leader in military might and space technology. Japan, on the other hand, was to become an aggressor nation in World War II, attempting to create her own **Co-Prosperity Sphere** in East Asia, in order to supply her growing population and *zaibatsu*-dominated economy. Whereas the war led to the creation of a Russian communist "empire" in eastern Europe, it led to the loss of all Japan's overseas territories.

During the **Cold War**, the Soviet Union exported its political and economic system to eastern Europe and set itself up as a model of socialist development for countries of the **Third World**. Japan, on the other hand, underwent its second major political and social transformation in less than a century, as American occupation forces imported democratic parliamentary institutions and American business methods (which the Japanese were to adapt and improve upon) and helped the country recover from its wartime devastation. Economic prosperity and world technological leadership followed. This chapter compares the development and problems of the two countries from the 1960s through the 1980s, including the break-up of the Soviet Union and the beginning of the slowdown of Japanese economic growth. In the end, Spodek concludes, both systems were successful to a point (the Japanese much more so than the Soviets'), but both had to face severe internal pressures and contradictions. In addition, while both countries systems were exported and copied (the Russians' forcibly so, in eastern Europe; while the "**Asian Tigers**" were to model themselves on Japan), neither system was completely adaptable to foreign soil: each was unique to its own society and time.

CAHPTER OUTLINE

A. The Contrasting Experiences of Russia and Japan

B. Russia: 1914-1990s

  1. The build-up to revolution
  2. Lenin and the Russian Revolution
      a. the Revolution of 1905
      b. March and October revolutions, 1917
  3. State planning, 1920-53
      a. Stalin's Five-Year Plans
      b. growth of Russian industry
  4. Women workers in the Soviet Union
  5. Exporting the revolution
  6. Russian state power and oppression
      a. Stalin's purges of the party leadership
      b. The "Gulag Archipelago"
  8. Khrushchev, Brezhnev, and Gorbachev
      a. de-Stalinization under Khrushchev
      b. Brezhnev and the arms race with the U.S.A.
      c. Gorbachev: *glastnost* and *perestroika*
      d. the collapse of the Soviet Union and the end of the Cold War

C. Japan: Fragile Superpower, 1914-1990s

  1. Before World War I
  2. Social consequences of wartime economic growth: the *zaibatsu*
  3. Militarism
  4. The run-up to the Pacific War, 1930-37: Manchuria
  5. The Pacific War, 1937-45
      a. the "Co-Prosperity Sphere"
      b. firebombing and defeat
  6. The Occupation, 1945-52
  7. Continuities, 1952-73: M.I.T.I.
  8. The "Oil Shocks" of 1973 and 1979
  9. International investment finance: 1989-1990s
  10. Social-economic-technological problems within Japan
      a. an aging society
      b. an overworked society
  11. Women in the workforce: differing perspectives
  12. Toward the future
  13. Japan as a model
      a. the "Asian Tigers"
      b. problems with the East Asian model

D. Conclusion

IDENTIFICATION TERMS

For each term provide an identification or definition, an approximate date, a geographical location (if relevant) and – most important – a concise explanation of its significance in the context of the question. (Page numbers from the text are provided for your reference.)

M.I.T.I. (p. 635):

Chernobyl (p. 624):

Co-Prosperity Sphere (p. 633):

"Asian Tigers" (pp. 640-641):

collectivization (p. 615-616):

Leon Trotsky (p. 614):

Czar Alexander II (p. 610):

zaibatsu (p. 629):

New Economic Policy (p. 614):

robotics (p. 639):

MULTIPLE CHOICE QUESTIONS

Select the response that completes the sentence or answers the question best.

1. The _____ was established by the Soviet Union in 1919 to spread communist revolution.
    a. Warsaw Pact
    b. Comintern
    c. Co-Prosperity Sphere
    d. Social Democratic Party

2. Japan's imperialist aggression in the 1930's was promoted mainly by which group?
    a. the army leadership
    b. the *zaibatsu*
    c. the samurai
    d. M.I.T.I.

3. According to Lenin's revolutionary theory, which group was to lead the coming revolution?
    a. professional revolutionaries
    b. the workers
    c. the peasant
    d. professional soldiers

4. As a result of the "Oil Shocks" of the 1970s, Japan:
    a. was plunged into a depression
    b. sent more foreign aid to oil producing countries
    c. drastically reduced its dependence on petroleum energy
    d. all of the above

5. While Nikita Khrushchev attacked Stalin's policies, he nevertheless sent Russian troops to quell an anti-Soviet uprising in _____ in 1956.
    a. Poland
    b. Chechnya
    c. Czechoslovakia
    d. Hungary

6. "TQM"– or "Total Quality Management – refers to a business management strategy imported by Japan from:
    a. Britain
    b. Germany
    c. France
    d. the United States

7. By the 1980s, women form the majority of professionals in the field of:
    a. medicine
    b. law
    c. engineering
    d. all of the above

8. Japan's economic system might best be described as:
   a. *laissez-faire* capitalism
   b. government-regulated capitalism
   c. state socialism
   d. a mixture of capitalism and socialism

9. The Soviet leader who was identified most closely with the call for exporting communism to other countries was:
   a. Leonid Brezhnev
   b. Leon Trotsky
   c. V. I. Lenin
   d. Josef Stalin

10. The phrase "dual economy," with respect to Japan, refers to the separation between:
    a. private enterprise and the government
    b. Japanese manufacturers and other East Asian countries
    c. factory laborers and robotics
    d. large-scale and smaller, local manufacturers

11. The Bolsheviks were able to seize and maintain control of Russia during the Russian revolution owing to:
    a. their ruthless use of terror and the *Cheka*, or secret police
    b. the efficient mobilization of the Red Army by Leon Trotsky
    c. their mobilization of popular support from peasants and workers
    d. all of the above

12. Which of the following has not been a major social problem in Japan since the 1970s?
    a. concern over the quality of Japanese public education
    b. industrial air and water pollution
    c. an overworked labor force
    d. an aging society

13. During the period of the Five-year Plans and collectivization in the Soviet Union, Josef Stalin mounted a brutal campaign against the *kulaks*. Who were they?
    a. wealthy peasants
    b. factory owners
    c. communist party dissidents
    d. supporters of the "Whites"

14. Japanese *zaibatsu* were similar in form and function to which type of European economic institution?
    a. labor unions
    b. guilds
    c. cartels
    d. banks

15. Russia's defeat by Japan in the war of 1904-1905 resulted in:
    a. the granting of democratic reforms by the Czar
    b. the origins of a revolutionary movement
    c. economic reforms
    d. all of the above

STUDY QUESTIONS

Consider the following questions carefully. Be prepared to supply specific evidence and examples to support your points in a class discussion or concise, well-organized written essay.

1. According to the text, Josef Stalin won the power struggle against Leon Trotsky after lenin's death – and then adapted Trotsky's programs. To what extent was this the case? Which programs, in particular, did Stalin "adapt"?

2. Why did Japan's plan to create a "Greater East Asia Co-Prosperity Sphere" fail, even before her defeat in World War II?

3. What were *glastnost* and *perestroika*? Why did Mikhail Gorbachev undertake them? Why did these reform policies lead to the break-up of the Soviet Union and the downfall of communism in Russia?

4. What were the goals of the United States' occupation of Japan under General Douglas MacArthur? What specific measures were undertaken to achieve them? How successful was the program, according to the text?

5. Compare the roles and status of women in the Soviet Union with those of Japanese women in the later post-war era (c. 1970-1990). In which society achieved fuller equality?

HOW DO WE KNOW?

The following questions are based on the various illustrations or quotations and extracts from primary source documents and historical interpretations in the chapter.

1. Describe the "East Asian Model" of economic development, as postulated by Ezra T. Vogel. To which countries has it been applied? What are the possible problems with the model, according to the text?

2. Describe the characteristics of "Socialist realism" in art? What purposes was it designed to serve? What techniques does it employ to serve those purposes? (Cite specific examples from the text.)

3. Using Josef Stalin's own words and those of his contemporaries (from the chapter), describe and explain his apparent goals and the methods which were used to achieve them.

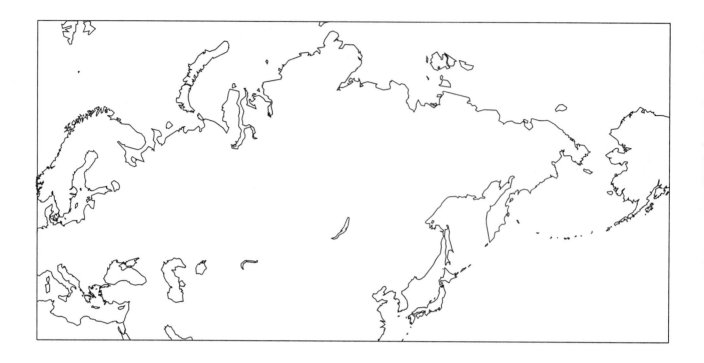

[The following exercise is based on the maps on pp. 619, 626 and 632]

On the map above, locate and identify the following:
1. Soviet "satellite" states in eastern Europe
2. the republics of the former Soviet Union
3. the Japanese imperial satellite state of Manchukuo

MULTIPLE CHOICE ANSWER KEY

1.	B	(618)	6.	D	(635)	11.	C	(614)
2.	A	(629-630)	7.	A	(618)	12.	A	(636-639)
3.	A	(613)	8.	B	(637)	13.	A	(616)
4.	C	(632)	9.	B	(618)	14.	C	(629)
5.	D	(623)	10.	D	(627)	15.	D	(613-614)

20   CHINA AND INDIA

1914 – 1997

THE GIANT AGRARIAN
NATION-WORLDS

COMMENTARY

Like Russia and Japan, the subjects of Chapter 20 – China and India – lend themselves quite well to comparative analysis, and the present unit is another fine example of **comparative history**. The major theme of the chapter is the different paths taken by the two nations, starting from very similar positions, in pursuit of the same goals: national unification and independence, political stability, economic development, technological modernization, social justice, and international respect and recognition. In both countries, the problems to be overcome have been enormous, and their struggles have consumed the entire 20ᵗʰ century, have often been violent and divisive, and are still continuing as a new millennium approaches.

As Howard Spodek points out, the historical, structural, and "environmental" similarities between the two societies are striking. They are two of the oldest and culturally influential civilizations in the world. Geographically, both encompass huge areas, constituting virtual sub-continents. They are the two most populous nations in the world, each with a population of approximately one billion inhabitants; and both of those populations exhibit enormous ethnic and linguistic diversity within a surprisingly uniform culture. Although both countries have many large cities and highly industrialized regions, they are still overwhelmingly rural, agrarian societies. At the beginning of the 20ᵗʰ century, both countries suffered under foreign domination and exploitation and both secured independence from that domination in the late 1940s, under the leadership of a dedicated, astute, and **charismatic** leader: **Mao Zedong** in China and **Mohandas Gandhi** in India. Since then, the leadership of both nations has had to confront the daunting problems of overpopulation, health and education, technological and economic development, and environmental pollution; tasks which have been further complicated in both cases by serious internal philosophical and ideological disagreements regarding the proper strategies to be pursued. In addition, there has been enormous popular resistance at times to government programs that have conflicted with centuries-old traditions and institutions. Finally, despite their respective adherence to the two major western political-economic systems – **Marxian communism** in the case of China and **parliamentary democracy** in the case of India – both nations have adapted those systems to their own, unique cultural and social conditions and have succeeded in becoming fully independent and very powerful members of the global community.

It is in the process of their political evolution and the specifics of their respective social and economic problems that the two nations differ most noticeably, and it is these differences that form much of the historical narrative in the chapter. First of all, China and India differ markedly in their relationship with the West. Unlike India, which was under British political control and cultural influence for almost 150 years, China was never completely subordinated to colonial rule. Consequently, much of the political discourse in India has centered around how much western influence to retain or reject, while in China it has tended to focus on how much to accept and adapt. Both countries achieved nation-state status through powerful mass movements led by well-organized political parties; but while the tactics of the **Indian National Congress** were those of political negotiation and non-violent resistance (**satyagraha**), those of the **Chinese Communist Party** were essentially those of peasant revolution and civil war. The communist victory in 1949 effected a resumption of China's long history of bureaucratic centralization and political unity, after the fragmentation of the early 20ᵗʰ century. India, on the other hand, split in two (Hindu India and Muslim **Pakistan**) at the time of independence, in keeping with its history of political disunity. (Pakistan itself split in 1972, with the independence of its eastern region, **Bangladesh**.) China pursued development through centralized state planning, highly authoritarian government, and Mao's version of Marxian communism. India adopted a pluralistic democracy, with a mixed capitalist-socialist economic system, and a federal form of government that allowed its various regions and ethnic groups a relatively high degree of autonomy. And while China at first aligned itself with the Soviet Union and the communist bloc and then swung around to a position of uncompromising hostility toward Russia and much closer economic and international ties with its former foe, the United States; India has maintained a much more consistent policy of "non-alignment" and, especially under the leadership of **Jawaharlal Nehru** and his daughter, **Indira Gandhi**, attempted to establish itself as the leader of the nations of the **Third World**. And the differences continue today, as well. Both nations have achieved noteworthy successes – China with its rapid technological transformation and prodigious economic growth under **Deng Xiaoping**; India with its "green revolution" and ability to feed its huge population – and both face severe challenges in the 21st century. For China, however, these problems are in some ways the consequences of its success so far. There is a growing movement for more political freedom and a growing disparity in wealth between the industrial cities on the coast and the agricultural interior. In India, as Spodek notes, the problems mostly stem from unsolved problems (Gandhi's "nightmares"): religious and regional separatism; overpopulation and unemployment; continuing class divisions and a growing disparity between the rich and poor; and massive illiteracy in an increasingly complicated technological world.

CHAPTER OUTLINE

A.   Introduction: "Nation-Worlds" Compared

B.   China, 1911-1990s

    1.   The 1911 Revolution: Sun Yat-sen
    2.   Power struggles, 1925-1937: Chiang Kai-shek (Jiang Jieshi)
    3.   Mao Zedong and the Rise of the Communist Party
        a.   Mao and peasant revolution
        b.   gender issues
        c.   the Long March and the rise to power, 1937-1949
    4.   Economic revolution, 1949-1966: the "Great Leap Forward"
    5.   The "Great Proletarian Cultural Revolution"
    6.   Economic recovery, 1970-1990s
        a.   Deng Xiaoping and industrial growth
        b.   the "Four Modernizations" (and #5 - democracy?)
    7.   China and the world, 1950-1990s

C.   India, 1914-1990s

    1.   The Indian National Congress and the independence struggle, 1914-1947
    2.   New political directions and reform: Mohandas Gandhi
        a.   Gandhi's philosophy and tactics
        b.   Opposition to Gandhi's views in India
    3.   India's problems and Gandhi's programs
        a.   Hindu-Muslim unity
        b.   abolition of untouchability
        c.   cultural policies: maintenance of Indian cultural traditions
        d.   prohibition (of alcohol)
        e.   technology and its dangers
    4.   The debate over technology: Gandhi vs. Nehru
    5.   Independence and after
        a.   "balkanization" – Pakistan and Bangladesh; the Punjab
        b.   socialism vs. capitalism
    6.   Gender issues
    7.   Economic, social and technological change since independence: seven problems
    8.   International relations since 1947

IDENTIFICATION TERMS

For each term provide an identification or definition, an approximate date, a geographical location (if relevant) and – most important – a concise explanation of its significance in the context of the chapter. (Page numbers are provided for your reference.)

"Four Modernizations" (p. 659):

Third World (p. 645)

Indira Gandhi (p. 674):

Taiwan (pp. 655 & 660):

satyagraha (p. 666):

Long March (p. 654):

harijan (p. 669):

Guomindang (p. 647):

Bangladesh (p. 671):

Living Thoughts of Chairman Mao (p. 658):

MULTIPLE CHOICE QUESTIONS

Select the response that completes the sentence or answers the question best.

1. After the death of Mao Zedong in 1976, the new Chinese leadership called for reforms, including greater freedom of expression, a restoration of cultural, educational and economic exchange with the outside world and:
   a. an economy more attuned to market principles
   b. restoration of friendly relations with the Soviet Union
   c. diplomatic connections with the United States
   d. all of the above

2. The Government of India Act of 1919 was a British parliamentary law which established a system known as _____, by which powers over agriculture, public works, education, and local government were transferred to elected Indian legislators.
   a. *swaraj*
   b. *dyarchy*
   c. *ahimsa*
   d. *jajmani*

3. An ongoing tension among the Chinese Communist leadership under Mao Zedong stemmed from policy disagreements between:
   a. advocates of industrial development and advocates of agricultural development
   b. advocates of ideological purity and advocates of realistic policies
   c. advocates of grass-roots populism and advocates of bureaucratic rule
   d. all of the above

4. One of the most controversial political issues in India since the 1950s has been the question of "protective discrimination" – the reservation of a certain quota of government positions for:
   a. Muslims
   b. Hindus
   c. untouchables
   d. women

5. The three principles of "nationalism, democracy, and livelihood" are most closely associated with which Chinese revolutionary leader?
   a. Sun Yat-sen
   b. Jiang Jieshi
   c. Mao Zedong
   d. Deng Xiaoping

6. The traditional Hindu precept of _____ , or "non-violence" was an important component of Gandhi's teaching and tactics.
   a. *satyagraha*
   b. *ashram*
   c. *swaraj*
   d. *ahimsa*

7. The founder of the Muslim League and first leader of Pakistan, this Indian leader broke with the Indian National Congress because he feared discrimination against Muslims in an independent India.
   a. Chandra Bose
   b. Tilak
   c. Jinnah
   d. Tagore

8. Mao's campaign in the late 1950s to encourage rural self-sufficiency and small-scale industrialization was called:
    a. the "Hundred Flowers"
    b. "Appropriate Technology"
    c. the "Great Leap Forward"
    d. the "Cultural Revolution"

9. Jiang Jieshi lost much popular during the civil war in China because:
    a. the Guomindang became very corrupt
    b. he was willing to negotiate with Japanese invaders
    c. he was identified with foreign business interests and Christian missionaries
    d. all of the above

10. The most serious problem with education in India today is:
    a. a lack of university-trained professionals and technicians
    b. an imbalance between primary education and higher education
    c. discrimination against women and untouchables in the educational system
    d. insufficient funding for universities

11. The Communists' policy of promoting gender equality in China was most effective in the area of:
    a. fostering more equality for women in the labor force and in the military
    b. creating more positions for women in the party leadership
    c. legislation against arranged marriages and the purchase of brides
    d. legislation dictating "one family, "one child"

12. A key aspect of Gandhi's policy of promoting Indian cultural traditions was:
    a. advocating that all Indians wear traditional clothing, as he did
    b. advocating the adoption of the Hindi language for education at all levels
    c. advocating the adoption of Hinduism as the national religion
    d. advocating the abolition of traditional caste distinctions

13. Which of the following was not a cause of the split between the governments of China and the Soviet Union?
    a. differences in communist ideology
    b. Soviet policy changes under Khrushchev
    c. the death of Mao Zedong
    d. disputes regarding the Russian-Chinese border

14. Jawaharlal Nehru disagreed with Gandhi most vigorously over the question of:
    a. the use of non-violent tactics to gain independence
    b. the adoption of socialism, rather than capitalism, in India
    c. the type of technology and scale of development appropriate for India
    d. the question of religious toleration in India

15. After independence, India established a federal-style government, with the boundaries of the states drawn to correspond most closely to:
    a. the homelands of various religious groups
    b. the concentrations of various ethnic and linguistic groups
    c. the borders of the old Indian principalities
    d. none of the above

Consider each of the following questions carefully. Be prepared to supply specific evidence and examples to support your points in a class discussion or concise, well-organized written essay.

1. India's economy could best be described as a mixture of capitalism and socialism, reflecting the philosophy of the Indian national Congress under Nehru and the fact the neither communism nor free-market capitalism has been able to win overwhelming support in the country. According to the author, what characteristics of communism and capitalism, respectively, might have inhibited their popularity in India?

2. In what respects did the policy of the "Four Modernizations" under Deng Xiaoping reflect the victory of the "bureaucratic realist" wing of the CCP over the ideological "Reds"? In what ways, however, did the new policy tend to de-stabilize China?

3. Compare the changes in the status of women in China and India since the 1940s. Which government has been more successful in achieving its stated goal of gender equality? What specific problems has each government tried to address? What factors have affected their success?

4. According to the author of the text, what are the most serious problems facing India today? How and with what degree of success is the Indian government addressing these problems?

5. Explain *satyagraha*. What were its major aspects? Why did Gandhi consider it the best tactic to achieve his goals for India? How did he reinforce the policy with regard to his own behavior? How effective was it, ultimately, in achieving his goals?

6. (This is a comparative question for students who have read the chapters on China and India (7 and 8) in Volume I of *The World's History*.) On page 185 of Volume I, Howard Spodek argues that, "During this time [c. 200 B.C.E . to 910 C.E.] China created political and cultural forms that would last for another thousand years, and, as we shall see in Chapter 20, perhaps even today." To what "forms" could he be referring? In what respects is the current government and society of China very similar to that of the Han and T'ang Dynasties, the Revolutions of 1911 and 1949 notwithstanding? Could the same statement be made, in some respects, about the India of today and the India of the Mauryas and the Guptas?

HOW DO WE KNOW?

The following questions are based on the various illustrations or quotations and extracts from primary source documents and historical interpretations in the text.

1. How did Mao Zedong's revolutionary philosophy and economic policies differ from those of Karl Marx, V. I. Lenin and Josef Stalin? How do you account for the differences in these communist viewpoints? (Cite specific evidence and quotations from Marx, Lenin, Stalin and Mao Zedong to support your points.

2. Explain the concept of "appropriate technology" and discuss its relationship to policy debates regarding industrialization and development in both China and India. What would sort of technology was considered "appropriate" for China by Mao Zedong? For India, by Mohandas Gandhi?

MAP ANALYSIS

The exercise below is based on the maps on pp. 652 and 672.

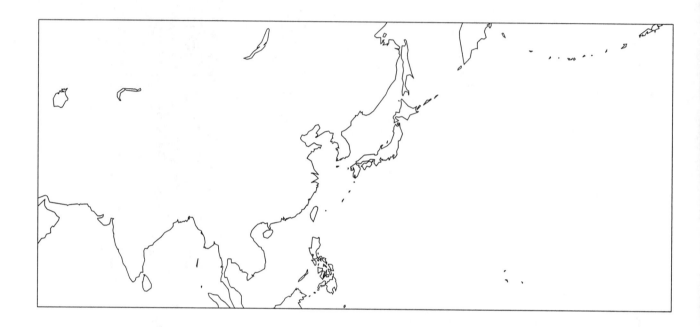

On the map above, locate and label the following:
1. areas of China which were controlled by the Japanese Army in 1944
2. areas of China which were under Chinese Communist control by 1945
3. the route of the Long march of 1934-35
4. the cities of Beijing, Chongqing, Yan'an, Shanghai, and Guangzhou
5. the islands of Taiwan and Hong Kong
6. areas of India which are claimed by China
7. the boundaries of India, Pakistan, and Bangladesh
8. the regions or states of Kashmir, the Punjab, Assam, and Tibet

MULTIPLE CHOICE ANSWER KEY

1.	A	(658)	6.	D	(666)	11.	A	(653-654)
2.	B	(662)	7.	C	(666)	12.	B	(669)
3.	D	(passim)	8.	C	(658)	13.	C	(660)
4.	C	(669)	9.	D	(650-655)	14.	C	(670)
5.	A	(647-648)	10.	B	(676)	15.	B	(672)

21   THE ARAB WORLD AND ITS NEIGHBORS
1880s – 1990s

NATIONALISM AND TECHNOLOGY
IN WEST ASIA AND NORTH AFRICA

COMMENTARY

Chapter 21 surveys the recent history of the region usually referred to as "the **Middle East**" – an Eurocentric (and generally inaccurate) term denoting the area encompassing North Africa, the eastern Mediterranean, and southwest Asia. "Arab World" is actually not much more satisfactory either, since the region includes Iranians, Azeris, Jews, Armenians, **Kurds**, Turks, Greeks, Berbers, and many other ethnic and linguistic groups, as well; although Arabs form the majority in the area. The chapter examines the development of seven of the twenty-odd nations of the region – Turkey, Egypt, Iraq, Iran, Algeria and Israel – and focuses on six themes common to all of those countries, and to the region as a whole.

The first theme is "nationalist struggles against colonialism and neocolonialism" (679), by which Spodek is referring not only to rebellions against Turkish rule in Arabia, for example, and the Egyptian nationalist movement against British rule and anti-French **Algerian Revolution**, but also the **Arab-Israeli conflict**, which many Arabs view as a struggle against European colonialism, in the form of **Zionism**.

The second theme is "attempts to maintain government stability," an especially difficult task in a region rent by religious, ethnic, ideological, and even tribal, divisions. Revolutions, military coups, terrorism, and assassination have been common occurrences in the region throughout the century, event from which even the most stable nations in the area, Israel and Saudi Arabia, have not been immune. Because of the region's chronic instability, most countires maintain very large military establishments, spending more, per capita, on defense than most other countries of the world. With such large armies, the possibility of a military coup or military dictatorship is an ever-present threat, and indeed, Turkey, Iraq, Egypt and Algeria have been under military domination for much of their history as independent states.

The "impact of oil resources" is another theme, especially for Saudi Arabia, Iraq and Kuwait (which is discussed briefly). As Spodek points out, oil revenues have not only had a direct impact on the development of the major producers in the region, providing billions of dollars for technological and institutional modernization (not to mention military expenditures), but they have had wider effects as well. In the 1970s **OPEC** (the Saudi-led Organization of Petroleum Exporting Countries) exerted a major influence on world affairs. The major oil-producing states of Arabia and the Persian Gulf region have been a magnet for immigration from Egypt and other Muslim countries, and the surplus wealth that Saudis, Kuwaitis, and others have invested abroad has greatly affected their foreign policies; generally exerting a moderating influence.

The region has also been an arena for competition among a number of "differing philosophies and methods of regional development," from the more radical **Pan-Arabism** of **Nasser**'s Egypt (embraced today by Muammar Qaddafi in Libya) and "**Arab Socialism**" of the *Baath* movement in Iraq and Syria; to the secular nationalism of **Ataturk's** Turkey and **Reza Pahlavi's** Iran; to the conservative Islamic monarchies of Saudi Arabia and the smaller Gulf States. With the Iranian Revolution led by the **Ayatollah Khomeini** in Iran in 1979, **religious fundamentalism** became established as yet another competing political movement and today almost every country in the region is affected by political movements seeking to establish a **theocratic** government in their nation. Egypt and Algeria are the msot affected at the present, but there are Islamic extremists in Turkey, Saudi Arabia, and the smaller Gulf States as well. Even Israel is affected, as the **ultra-Orthodox** Jewish parties have increased their strength and the country has begun to experience terrorist attacks against Arabs and Israeli moderates, including the assassination of Prime Minister **Yitzhak Rabin**. The resurgence of religion in the politics of the region has further clouded the future of Arab-Israeli relations and complicated all attempts at regional cooperation and organization.

CHAPTER OUTLINE

A. The Middle East and North Africa: Outstanding Issues

B. Turkey

    1. The end of the Ottoman Empire: Mustafa Kemal
    2. The rise of secular nationalism in Turkey, 1923-1990s
        a. Ataturk and modernization
        b. government alteration between democracy and military dictatorship
        c. NATO membership and western alignment

C. Egypt

    1. British rule, 1882-1952
        a. The *Wafd* vs. the Muslim Brotherhood
        b. Nasser and non-alignment
    2. Technological innovation, 1956-1990s
        a. the high Aswan Dam project and the Suez Crisis, 1956
        b. Egypt and Israel
        c. problems and progress in Egypt today

D. The Persian Gulf: Oil, Religion, and Politics

E. Iraq, 1939-1990s

    1. The *Baath* Party and "Arab Socialism"
    2. Saddam Hussein
        a. the Iran-Iraq War, 1980-88
        b. invasion of Kuwait and the Gulf War, 1990-91

F. Iran, 1970-1990s

    1. Shah Reza Pahlavi and modernization
    2. The rise of Ayatollah Khomeini
        a. the Islamic Revolution, 1979
        b. Iran and the world, 1979-1997
        c. Islamic law and domestic policies

G. Saudi Arabia

    1. Ibn Saud
    2. OPEC and development
    3. moderation in foreign policy

H. North Africa: Algeria

    1. The movement toward independence
    2. The Algerian Revolution and after

I. Israel

    1. Israel and the Arab World: <u>How do we assess significance</u>?
    2. The creation of Israel, 1948
    3. The Arab-Israeli conflict

IDENTIFICATION TERMS

For each term provide an identification or definition, an approximate date, a geographical location (if relevant) and – most important – a concise explanation of its significance in the context of the chapter. (Page numbers from the text are provided for your reference.)

Baath **Party** (pp. 691-692):

kibbutzim (p. 703):

Aswan Dam (pp. 688-689):

The Wretched of the Earth (p. 700):

Ibn Saud (p. 695):

Balfour Declaration (pp. 701-702):

Ayatollah Khomeini (p. 694):

Palestine Liberation Organization (p. 704):

Armenian Massacres (p. 682):

Anwar Sadat (pp. 689-690):

MULTIPLE CHOICE QUESTIONS

Select the response that completes the sentence or answers the question best.

1. Anwar Sadat, Nasser's successor as leader of Egypt, signed a peace agreement with Israel in 1978, principally because:
    a. of diplomatic pressure from the United States
    b. Egyptian forces had been beaten in every war with the Israelis
    c. the Soviet Union had with drawn its military support
    d. maintaining a wartime military establishment had simply become too expensive

2. The United States and Britain supported a military coup in Iran to overthrow the government of Prime Minister Mussadeg, because:
    a. he had violated human rights
    b. he had nationalized the Iranian oil industry
    c. he had disagreed with the Shah of Iran
    d. he had launched an attack on Iraq

3. Among Israel's current social problems are:
    a. tensions between the country's orthodox religious minority and the majority of secular Jews
    b. tensions between Ashkenazi Jews from Europe and Sephardic Jews from the Mediterranean area
    c. assimilation of new immigrants from Russia and eastern Europe
    d. all of the above

4. In the Sykes-Picot Agreement in 1916, the governments of Britain and France:
    a. agreed to the establishment of an Arab state in return for Arab support against the Ottoman Empire in World War I
    b. agreed to the Zionist pleas for the establishment of a "Jewish homeland" in Palestine
    c. agreed to divide the Middle East between themselves after World War I
    d. agreed to the establishment of a Palestinian state

5. Mustafa Kemal (Ataturk), who initiated a thorough series of modernizing reforms in Turkey, was supported in these efforts primarily by the _____, whom he considered to be the "true owners" of the country.
    a. the Turkish army
    b. the Muslim religious elites
    c. the urban workers
    d. the intelligentsia of lawyers, engineers, teachers and doctors

6. The polices pursued by Gamel Abdel Nasser of Egypt included pan-Arab unity, Arab socialism, technological modernization, a strong military establishment and:
    a. alliance with the Soviet Union
    b. alliance with the United States
    c. alignment with India and other Third World nations
    d. alliance with Britian and France

7. OPEC countries such as Saudi Arabia, Kuwait, and other Persian Gulf oil states have been reluctant to increase oil prices in recent years, for fear of:
    a. military retaliation by the oil consuming countries
    b. trade restrictions by the oil consuming countries
    c. terrorist attacks by Iran and Iraq
    d. doing economic damage to their own financial investments in the oil consuming countries

8. France fiercely resisted granting Algeria independence in the 1950s, primarily because:
   a. of the value of Algerian oil production
   b. of the fear that Algeria would become an ally of the Soviet union
   c. of the large number of French settlers in Algeria
   d. of the help the Algerian rebels were receiving from Nasser in Egypt

9. The Zionist movement found its greatest support among Jews in which of the following areas before World War II?
   a. Russia and eastern Europe
   b. France, Germany and western Europe
   c. Britain and the United States
   d. North Africa and the Middle East

10. Until 1952, Egyptian nationalist efforts to gain independence from Britain were opposed by:
    a. Israel
    b. the Egyptian army
    c. the United States
    d. religious conservatives within Egypt

11. Which of the following groups have not been persecuted as a group by Saddam Huseein of Iraq?
    a. Shi'ite Muslims
    b. Sunni Muslims
    c. Jews
    d. Kurds

12. Opponents of the forced modernization programs of Shah Reza Pahlavi in Iran included the Shi'ite religious establishment, left-wing intellectuals and:
    a. the Iranian army
    b. the United States government
    c. oil companies, which were heavily taxed and regulated
    d. urban residents, who suffered from inflation and unemployment

13. Which of the following is not a reason why the government of Saudi Arabia has maintained close ties with the United States and the west over the years?
    a. fear of attacks by its militaristic neighbors
    b. fear of Islamic fundamentalism within its borders
    c. the need for economic aid from the west
    d. conservative suspicion of pan-Arab nationalist and Arab socialist movements

14. The "Palestinian Question" in Arab-Israeli relations became more serious:
    a. as a result of Israeli independence in 1948
    b. as a result of the 1973 war between Israel and the Arab states
    c. as a result of the Israeli occupation of the West Bank after the Six-Day War in 1967
    d. as a result of the Gulf War in 1991

15. Besides Israel, the only nation in the region in which a woman has become Prime Minister and head of government is:
    a. Iran
    b. Egypt
    c. Turkey
    d. Algeria

STUDY QUESTIONS

Consider each of the following questions carefully. Be prepared to supply specific evidence and examples to support your points in a class discussion or concise, well-organized written essay.

1. What are the various "emplotments" or ways of looking at the Arab-Israeli Conflict, according to the text? How do these different views reinforce each other? Which "plot" is most likely to be accepted by Israelis? By Arabs?

2. In the 20th century history of many of the Muslim countries of the region, there have often been odd alliances of different groups, such as fundamentalist Muslim religious leaders and left-wing intellectuals on the one hand, and conservative monarchies and progressive technocrats on the other. How can one explain these "strange bedfellows"?

3. One interpretation of the seemingly irrational and aggressive behavior of Saddam Huseein in Iraq is that many of his actions are motivated out of fear. According to the text, which take this position, who does Saddam Hussein fear, and why?

4. Mustafa Kemal (Ataturk) in Turkey was, in many ways, a model for modernizing leaders in the Muslim world. Discuss his policies and draw comparisons with his goals and methods and those of later modernizers. Provide specific examples from at least two different countries.

HOW DO WE KNOW?

The following questions are based on the various illustrations or quotations and extracts from primary source documents and historical interpretations in the chapter.

1. The High Aswan Dam in Egypt was important to Nasser and the Egyptian people for a number of reasons. Explain its economic and <u>political</u> importance, based on your reading of Nasser's own explanation (pp. 688-689).

2. Many Islamic fundamentalists, such as the Ayatollah Khomeini in Iran, rejected parliamentary democracy just as strongly as they rejected military dictatorship. On what grounds did Khomeini argue against democracy? Under his theocratic system, who would actually rule the country?

MAP ANALYSIS

The exercise below is based on the maps on pp. 680, 682 and 705.

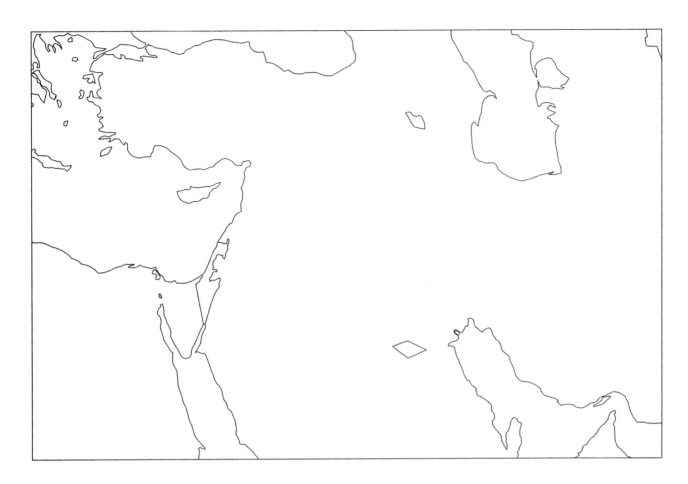

On the map above locate and identify the following:

1. the nations which were (or are) led by the following men: Ataturk, Nasser, Reza Pahlavi, Saddam Hussein
2. the country whose ruling family led the revolt against the Ottoman Empire in World War I
3. two countries with large Shi'ite Muslim populations
4. the area affected directly by the Balfour Declaration of 1917
5. and the following "flashpoints" – areas of military conflict and the dates of those conflicts: the Suez Canal, the Persian Gulf, the West Bank, Kuwait, the Gaza Strip

MULTIPLE CHOICE ANSWER KEY

1.	D	(689)	6.	C	(688)	11.	B	(692)
2.	B	(693)	7.	D	(698)	12.	D	(695)
3.	D	(705-706)	8.	C	(699)	13.	C	(699)
4.	C	(690)	9.	A	(702)	14.	C	(704)
5.	A	(683)	10.	D	(686)	15.	C	(685)

22   SUB-SAHARAN AFRICA
1914 – 1990s

COLONIALISM, INDEPENDENCE,
AND THEIR AFTERMATH

COMMENTARY

    Chapter 22 takes on the daunting task of attempting to survey and analyze the history of the world's second largest continent during the 20th century. This is a particularly difficult task, owing to what might be termed Africa's "three-dimensional diversity." Spodek cites the first dimension of this diversity in the chapter's introduction, where he discusses the multiplicity of ethnic groups and cultural traditions in Sub-Saharan Africa, as well as the vast differences in territorial extent, population size, literacy rates, life expectancy, **gross national product**, and **per capita income** within the various countries of the region. The other two dimensions are discussed less explicitly, as recurring themes throughout the chapter. One is the different imperial policies of the European colonial powers, which were to have a strong impact on their respective colonies' transition to independence. In terms of political infrastructure, it was the British colonies which were generally the best prepared for self-rule, as a result of the pragmatic institution-building policies of the colonizers. France, on the other hand, had generally accorded Africans and their culture much more respect and had encouraged assimilation to French ways as well. As a result, the former colonies of France have generally retained close ties with their former "mother country." The brutally exploitative rule of the Belgians in the Congo (now **Zaire**) and the Portuguese in **Angola** and **Mozambique** left those countries poorly prepared for independence and torn by internal strife. The third dimension of diversity comprises the divergent paths taken by the new leadership of the emerging nations of Sub-Saharan Africa after independence. A few, like the former French colony of **Cote d'Ivoire** (Ivory Coast), chose a capitalist economic system and close connections with France and the world economy. **Kwame Nkrumah** of **Ghana**, on the other hand, advocated a form of **state socialism**, with government ownership of the major productive industries and large-scale development projects. Other countries, like **Tanzania**, under the leadership of **Julius Nyerere**, tried to develop an economic system based on traditional African communalism. Some nations, particularly Zaire and many former French colonies, sought economic and military aid from Europe and the United States, while others sought aid from the Soviet Union and even communist Cuba. Finally, there was **South Africa**, a unique case in that it was the only white-dominated government in the region after 1976.

    In order to try to reach some tentative conclusions, the text adopts a selective approach, comparing development in a number of representative countries, in an attempt to answer several crucial questions. The first question the author addresses is, essentially, "How did European colonialism work?" What were its salient economic and administrative features, both generally and in selected colonies. A second issue, addressed in more detail, is how Africans were able to mobilize and organize broad-based opposition to colonial rule and why, ultimately, the European colonial powers were forced to accede to their demands for independence. The second half of the chapter deals with the post-independence era and asks the questions, "[W]hat political, economic and social systems did African peoples implement to rule themselves" and "How well were these systems working – or not working and why?" (Spodek, 708-709). An important aspect of the latter question is the issue of the extent to which Africa's continuing political instability and economic underdevelopment is the result of the colonial legacy and continuing intervention by external forces (**neocolonialism**), as opposed to unrealistic choices made by Africans themselves or the greed and corruption of some of their leaders. Finally, the author addresses the question of the survival of African cultural traditions and the extent to which they impact on the societies of Africa and the world today.

CHAPTER OUTLINE

A. Introduction: Important Questions

B. To World War I: Colonialism Established

    1. European encroachment and resistance
    2. Economic investment
    3. Colonial administration

C. Colonialism Challenged: 1914-1957

    1. The World Wars and the weakening of European control
    2. Origins of the independence movements: political and educational
    3. Seeds of discontent: social, cultural and religious
    4. Pan-Africanism, 1914-45

D. Winning Independence: 1945-1975

    1. British colonies: Ghana, Nigeria, Kenya
    2. French colonies
    3. Belgian colonies: the Congo Crisis
    4. Portuguese colonies
    5. Southern Rhodesia (Zimbabwe)

E. South Africa

    1. The Union of South Africa (1910)
    2. *Apartheid* (1948)
    3. Nelson Mandela and the African National Congress
    4. F. W. de Klerk and the transition to majority rule

F. Evaluating the Legacy of Colonialism

G. Independence and After

    1. Internal politics
    2. Altering borders
    3. Refugees and exiles
    4. Dictatorship and corruption

H. Economic Issues

    1. Socialism or capitalism? – searching for an African path to development
    2. Roots of the economic problems: an economic and historiographic debate
    3. Economic solutions

I. Cultural Life

    1. *Negritude*
    2. Music
    3. Cinema
    4. Literature

J. African History: <u>How Do We Know?</u>

IDENTIFICATION TERMS

      For each term provide an identification or definition, an approximate date, a geographical location (if relevant) and – most important – a concise explanation of its significance in the context of the chapter. (Page numbers from the text are provided for your reference.)

Nelson Mandela (pp. 723-725):

monoculture (p. 712):

Chinua Achebe (p. 740):

Kwame Nkrumah (passim):

Yaounde Convention (p. 721):

apartheid (p. 723):

Pan-African Congresses (p. 718):

Maji-Maji Revolt (p. 711):

Biafra (p. 728):

"Big Men" (p. 730):

MULTIPLE CHOICE QUESTIONS

Select the response that completes the sentence or answers the question best.

1. An important survival of traditional west African culture is the *griot*, which is a:
    a. custodian of folk history
    b. type of poem
    c. type of folk dance
    d. type of musical instrument

2. Apartheid and white minority rule in South Africa were finally brought to an end in the 1990s, by:
    a. worldwide economic and cultural sanctions on South Africa
    b. a change of leadership in the Afrikaner leadership
    c. political pressure, civil disobedience and guerrilla attacks by black South Africans
    d. all of the above

3. Until 1945, meetings of the Pan-African movement were held outside of Africa and were convened by:
    a. African-American leaders
    b. African leaders educated in European countries
    c. African leaders opposed to independence
    d. African leaders educated in communist countries

4. The economic difficulties of the Republic of Cote d'Ivoire in the 1980s demonstrate the problems inherent in:
    a. African forms of socialism
    b. the practice of monoculture
    c. neocolonialism
    d. inappropriate-scale technology

5. The most serious health problem facing Africa today is:
    a. the spread of the AIDS virus, through heterosexual contact
    b. malaria, caused by construction of many dams and reservoirs, which breed mosquitoes
    c. malnutrition, because foreign aid workers are coming under increasing attacks
    d. overpopulation, because the fertility rate continues to rise

6. Over 300,000 people were killed in Uganda and all Asian immigrants driven out of the country, during the dictatorship of:
    a. Samuel Doe
    b. Idi Amin
    c. Mobutu Sese Seko
    d. Jean-Bedel Bokassa

7. During the period of colonialism and the "Scramble for Africa," the only African country to successfully fight off attempts at European colonial control was:
    a. Ghana
    b. Mozambique
    c. Somalia
    d. Ethiopia

8. In the British colonies of eastern and southern Africa, significant positions in local trade and commerce were often occupied by:
    a. cadres of trained African professionals
    b. English immigrants
    c. Indian immigrants
    d. appointed African chiefs

9. Which of the following countries has <u>not</u> experienced severe tribal conflict since it has become independent?
    a. Nigeria
    b. Ghana
    c. Rwanda
    d. Uganda

10. Which of the following countries supported guerrilla forces or "Big Men" dictators in Africa?
    a. France
    b. the United States
    c. Cuba
    d. all of the above

11. The white settler government of Southern Rhodesia (now Zimbabwe) resisted pressures to hand over governing power to native African leaders until:
    a. their government was overthrown by neighboring African countries
    b. the Portuguese left neighboring Mozambique
    c. they succumbed to economic pressures from outside Africa
    d. the South African government withdrew its support

12. British colonial administration was characterized by which of the following policies?
    a. indirect rule through local chiefs
    b. assimilation
    c. neocolonialism
    d. all of the above

13. African women often became involved in independence movements through their connection with:
    a. membership in labor unions
    b. protests against market taxes
    c. employment in the colonial civil service
    d. attendance at schools and universities

14. President Julius Nyerere of Tanzania sponsored which of the following strategies of economic development?
    a. local collectivized agriculture
    b. state-ownership
    c. appropriate-scale technology
    d. free-market capitalism

15. The Ghanaian historian Adu Boahen has argued that the most important factor in changing the minds of Europeans about the justice of colonialism was:
    a. the increasing expense of maintaining a colonial empire during the Depression
    b. the breakup of the German, Austrian, Ottoman and Russian empires at the end of World War I
    c. the Italian invasion of Ethiopia in 1935
    d. the granting of Indian independence in 1947

Consider each of the following questions carefully. Be prepared to supply specific evidence and examples to support your points in a class discussion or concise, well-organized written essay.

1. Although the leadership of African independence movements was almost always drawn from the tiny minority of European (or sometimes American) educated elites, historians have identified a number of local organizations which served as recruiting and training grounds for grass-roots support. Citing specific examples, identify at least three such organizations and explain how they served to promote support for independence.

2. Define "monoculture" and explain the various ways in which its practice has proven so harmful to African economies and the African environment. Since it was so harmful, why was it introduced in the first place?

3. What specific problems did African leaders confront in the years immediately following independence? How successful were various nations in dealing with these problems? To the extent that they were not successful, why was this the case?

4. What various types of economic systems were tried in Africa by the newly independent countries? How successful were the various experiments? What problems did they encounter?

5. How did the traumatic experiences of the two world wars and the Depression undermine the moral authority and confidence of the European nations to maintain colonial rule over African peoples? In what ways did they also undermine Europe's ability to maintain that control?

HOW DO WE KNOW?

The following questions are based on the various illustrations or quotations and extracts from primary source documents and historical interpretations in the chapter.

1. "Who's to blame?" Citing explanations and arguments from the various historians, economists, politicians and others discussed in this chapter, what or who is to blame for Africa's underdeveloped economies and unstable governments? Be sure to explain their respective arguments fully. Which arguments, in your view, are the most convincing?

2. Based on evidence in the chapter, how well did the French colonial policy of "assimilation" work? Is there any evidence that the former colonies and colonial subjects of France actually were "assimilated" into French culture?

3. Why did E. F. Schumacher's *Small Is Beautiful* attract such widespread acceptance in Africa? What is "appropriate" about "Appropriate Technology" in the African context?

MAP ANALYSIS

The exercise below is based on the maps on pp. 711, 714, and 719.

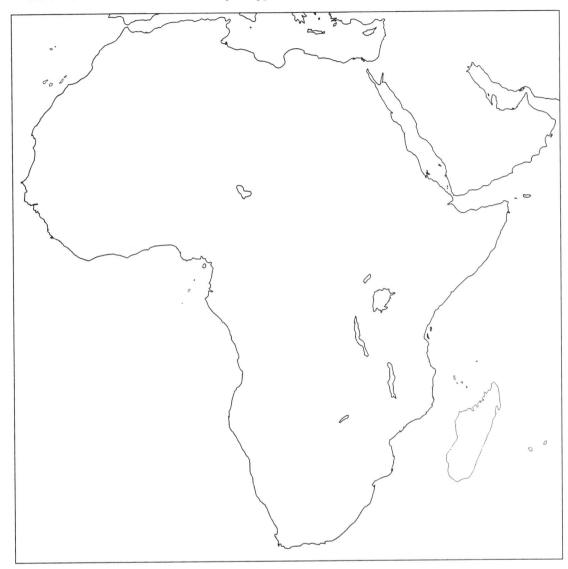

On the map above, locate and identify the following?

1. the respective colonial possessions of Britain, France, Germany, Italy, Belgium, and Portugal in 1914
2. the independent countries of Ghana, Uganda, Kenya, Zaire, Tanzania, Mali, Cote d'Ivoire (Ivory Coast), Sudan, and Mozambique
3. the only African country to successfully repel a European invasion before World War I
4. the economies with the greatest amount of mineral wealth in Africa
5. the countries that have experienced the most serious ethnic or tribal unrest since independence

MULTIPLE CHOICE ANSWER KEY (with page references)

1.	A	(738)	6.	B	(730)	11.	B	(722)
2.	D	(724-725)	7.	D	(711)	12.	A	(713)
3.	A	(717)	8.	C	(712)	13.	B	(717)
4.	B	(731)	9.	B	(passim)	14.	A	(730)
5.	A	(734)	10.	D	(730)	15.	C	(713)

23   LATIN AMERICA
1870 – 1990s

THE SEARCH FOR AN INTERNATIONAL
POLICY ON ECONOMICS AND TECHNOLOGY

COMMENTARY

The final chapter focuses on the nations of Latin America and their dual quest for economic development and political stability in the 20th century. In many ways, it is a region of contradictions. Although settled by Europeans, like North America and Australia, as a region it has been less prosperous and peaceful than those areas. While there is a broad foundation of cultural unity, Latin America, like India or the Arab world, remains politically fragmented. And while most of the countries of mainland Central and South America have been independent since the early 19th century (many of the islands of the **Caribbean** did not become independent until late in the 20th century), they are virtually all still struggling for true economic independence. And, though richly endowed with natural resources, their populations have not always enjoyed the full benefit of this abundance..

Most of these contradictions are the lingering results of the conditions of Latin America's colonization by Europeans during the 16th and 17th centuries and the circumstances of their independence in the 19th century. Unlike the British colonies of North America, where European settlers migrated in great numbers and filled the land with small and medium-farms, the Spanish, Portuguese, French and English colonists in Latin America and the Caribbean islands came in relatively small numbers, establishing much larger sugar and coffee plantations, sheep and cattle *estancias*, and gold and silver mines. There tended to be more intermarriage with the indigenous American population, and many more African slaves were imported to work the large agricultural and mining concerns than were sold to North American slave owners. Massive European immigration did not occur until the late 19th and early 20th centuries, and much of it went to Brazil, Uruguay, Argentina and Chile. The result is a rich mixture of American, African, and European cultures and races, but one in which the *creoles*, or descendants of the original Europeans who colonized the region, have maintained most of the wealth and political power. And they have not, it would seem, used either wisely. Rather than developing their own domestic industries, as North Americans did so effectively during the 19th century, the *creole* elites were content, as it were, to continue to live off the land and the fruits of the labor of their Amerindian, *mestizo*, and African employees and tenant farmers. The economic results of this underdevelopment were a grossly unequal distribution of wealth and the perpetuation of **neocolonial** status for the region, as most of the produce was sold to Europe and most investment capital (and what little industry there was) was controlled by European countries. After the immediate post-independence decade, no attempt was made at political unification, and the region remained politically divided and weak. The class-ridden social conditions resulted in frequent political unrest and government instability, which was usually quelled by military commanders – *caudillos* – who set themselves up as dictators; another trend that has continued down to the present day. Neither the tendency to political instability and *caudillismo* nor the burden of economic dependence has been particularly helped by the policies of the United States, which replaced Europe as Latin America's rich – and meddling – uncle after the First World War. American interventionist policies reached their height during the interwar period and again during the Cold War, as the United States repeatedly intervened to subvert or overthrow radical, populist leaders and reestablish conservative – often military – rule. At the present time, it appears that progress is being made on both the economic and political fronts, but Latin America's financial crisis of the early 1980's and continuing unrest in Mexico, Peru, Colombia, and recently in **Fidel Castro's** communist Cuba demonstrates that the battles are far from being won.

Chapter 23 reviews Latin America's economic and political struggles through an intensive comparative survey of four of its most important – and in many ways most typical – nations: Mexico, Brazil, Argentina, and Cuba.. It asks, and attempts to answer the questions of, "How did Latin America's problems originate?" "What reforms have been attempted?" and "What is the outlook for the future?"

CHAPTER OUTLINE

A. Latin American Diversity Today

B. Technology, Industrialization, and Latin American Elites: 1870-1916

    1. Foreign investments and primary production
    2. Immigration and social change

C. The Mexican Revolution: 1910-1920

    1. The dictatorship of Porfirio Diaz
    2. *Mestizo* revolutionaries: "Pancho" Villa and Emiliano Zapata
    3. Obregon and the revolutionary program
    4. Lazaro Cardenas: the revolution institutionalized
    5. Culture as a tool of revolution: Diego Rivera

D. Revolutionary Politics in the 1920s and 1930s: Peru and APRA

E. The Market Crash and Import Substitution, 1929-1960

    1. Import substitution (ISI)
    2. Militarism and democracy in Brazil: 1930-1990s
        a. Getulio Vargas and the "New State"
        b. Military dictatorship: "Order and Progress"
        c. Return to democracy
    3. Populism and nationalism in Argentina: 1920-1980
        a. Juan Peron and the *decamisados*
        b. Opinions from and about "Evita"

F. The United States and Latin America

    1. "Dollar Diplomacy" military and interventions, 1898-1934
    2. Guatemala, 1951-1990s
    3. Chile, 1970-1990
    4. Cuba, 1950-1990s
        a. Fidel Castro and the Cuban Revolution
        b. Che Guevara and guerrilla warfare
        c. Cuba, the U.S.A. and the Soviet Union, 1961-1991

G. Current Issues and Trends

    1. The military in power, 1960-1990
    2. Economics and technology
        a. "development" vs. "growth'
        b. the crisis of the 1980s
        c. NAFTA
        d. environmental issues
    3. Amerindians: oppression and response
    4. Religion and hope for the poor
        a. "Liberation Theology"
        b. the growth of evangelical Protestantism
    5. The "Unorganized Sector"

IDENTIFICATION TERMS

For each term provide an identification or definition, an approximate date, a geographical location (if relevant) and – most important – a concise explanation of its significance in the context of the chapter. Page numbers from the text are provided for your reference.

Rigoberta Menchu (pp. 769-770):

mestizos (pp. 749, 769):

Bay of Pigs (p. 763):

P.R.I. (pp. 753, 755)

"Good Neighbor Policy" (p. 762):

Eva Peron (p. 758-760):

Diego Rivera (pp. 750-751):

Salvadore Allende (p.762):

Lazaro Cardenas (pp. 753-754):

Che Guevara (p. 764):

MULTIPLE CHOICE QUESTIONS

Select the response that completes the sentence or answers the question best.

1. Evangelical Protestantism is the fastest-growing religion in Latin America, owing to the extended missionary effort from the United States, the movement's suitability to the increasingly urbanized society, and:
   a. its condemnation of communism
   b. the identification of the Catholic Church with the ruling elites
   c. the attraction of its "Liberation Theology"
   d. all of the above

2. Mexican revolutionary leader Emiliano Zapata's "Plan of Ayala" called for:
   a. the confiscation of all foreign owned industry
   b. continuous guerrilla warfare against the Mexican government
   c. the restoration of land to Indian villages
   d. the establishment of the Institutional Revolutionary Party (P.R.I.)

3. After the Cuban Revolution of 1959 and Fidel Castro's embracing of communism:
   a. the United States implemented the "Alliance for Progress"
   b. a number of Latin American governments were taken over by the military
   c. the U.S. attempted the military overthrow of Castro's government
   d. all of the above

4. Juan Peron ruled Argentina from 1946 to 1954, with the help of the Argentine Army, his charismatic wife, "Evita" and:
   a. the Roman Catholic Church
   b. the labor unions
   c. the United States
   d. wealthy landowners

5. Which of the following promises of Fidel Castro's six-point plan for Cuba did he fail to implment?
   a. industrial development and the end of reliance on sugar exports
   b. free medical services and improved health care
   c. improved education
   d. extensive land collectivization

6. Using the statistical measurements of life expectancy and *per capita* share of the gross national product, the poorest country in Latin America is:
   a. Guatemala
   b. Haiti
   c. Cuba
   d. Nicaragua

7. The third largest language group in Latin America today is composed of native speakers of:
   a. Portuguese
   b. English
   c. native American languages
   d. French

8. Brazil, under the dictatorship of Getulio Vargas, practiced which economic policy?
   a. import substitution
   b. neocolonialism
   c. communism
   d. primary industrialization

9. Rigoberta Menchu of Guatemala received the 1992 Nobel Peace Prize for her work and writing on behalf of:
   a. Guatemalan women
   b. Latin American laborers
   c. "Liberation Theology
   d. Guatemalan Indians

10. The last major series of social and economic reforms of the Mexican Revolution took place under the presidency of:
    a. Victoriano Huerta
    b. Emiliano Zapata
    c. Lazaro Cardenas
    d. Alvaro Obregon

11. The strategy of import substitution industrialization failed because:
    a. the development of new industries required importing expensive technology
    b. most of the benefits went to the urban middle classes instead of the workers
    c. the countries could not export enough products to pay for the capital investments
    d. all of the above

12. Vargas in Brazil and Peron in Argentina combined corporatist social policies and nationalism in ways similar to:
    a. the Soviet Union
    b. Cuba
    c. Italy and Germany
    d. the Mexican Revolution

13. Besides NAFTA, another free trade initiative between the United States and Mexico has been:
    a. joint assembly plants on the U.S. Mexico border
    b. American aid to Mexican banks
    c. large purchases of Mexican agricultural products by the United States
    d. cooperation with Mexican police to stop drug trafficking

14. The advocates of "Liberation Theology" claim to combine Christian ethics with:
    a. libertarian politics
    b. Marxist politics
    c. free enterprise economics
    d. land reform

15. The Mexican Revolution's most radical leaders, Francisco Villa and Emiliano Zapata represented which ethnic group?
    a. *creoles*
    b. Africans
    c. *mestizos*
    d. Amerindians

STUDY QUESTIONS

Consider each of the following questions carefully. Be prepared to supply specific evidence and examples to support your points in a class discussion or concise, well-organized written essay.

1. Explain ISI (Import Substitution Industrialization). How did the concept address Latin America's chronic economic problems? Why did it fail to achieve its goals?

2. Discuss the role of religion – "Liberation Theology" and evangelical Protestantism in particular – in Latin America since 1980. What reasons does the text give for the success of each? Why has "Liberation Theology" lost its earlier energy?

3. Lazaro Cardenas, Getulio Vargas, Juan Peron, and Fidel Castro have been among Latin America's most significant leaders in the 20th century. Compare their respective policies and programs. What did they have in common? Where did they differ?

4. Discuss U.S. policy in Latin America, from "Dollar Diplomacy" through the "Good Neighbor Policy" and the "Alliance for Progress," to NAFTA. What have been some of the effects of U.S. policies on the region? How was the United States able to exert its influence?

HOW DO WE KNOW?

The following questions are based on the various illustrations or quotations and extracts from primary source documents and historical interpretations in the chapter.

1. " Eva Peron and Rigoberta Menchu have been two of Latin America's most influential women in the 20th century. Although they were different in many ways, there were also strong similarities." Discuss this statement, with reference to the personal appeal and following of each of these women.

2. Compare the revolutionary tactics and philosophy of Che Guevara with those of Mao Zedong in China. How was each particularly suited to their environment?

3. How did Diego Rivera exemplify the programs and popular support of the Mexican Revolution in his art? What themes and imagery did he use to portray the ideals of the revolution?

MAP ANALYSIS

The following exercise is based on the maps on pp. 743 and 754.

Locate and identify the following on the map on p. 129.
1. the two countries with the highest per capita GNP in Latin America in 1995
2. the Latin American countries with substantial oil reserves
3. those countries which have <u>not</u> experienced right-wing military rule in the 20th century
4. those countries which experienced United States or U.S. supported military interventions
5. two of the *maquiladores* industrial centers
6. two countries with substantial mineral deposits

MULTIPLE CHOICE ANSWER KEY (with page references)

1.	B	(772)	6.	B	(745)	11.	D	(757)
2.	C	(749)	7.	C	(742)	12.	C	(757)
3.	D	(759, 763)	8.	A	(757)	13.	A	(768)
4.	B	(760)	9.	D	(770)	14.	B	(771)
5.	A	(763, 766)	10.	C	(755)	15.	C	(749)